T0154060

ON PURPOSE *with* PURPOSE

"Strap into the cockpit with "Rammer" and get ready for a double dose of purpose-centric inspiration! John, like no other individual I've met, lives and leads with purposefulness reflective of his Top Gun pilot training and beyond. In this book he'll take you on a flight into the wild blue yonder that will help propel you to develop a purposeful and impactful glidepath for your life!"

— **Drew Hiss**, Founder + CEO, Acumen, Author of *Sharpen*

"John translates his experiences in the cockpit of an F-14 and the boardroom of Fortune 100 companies, as well as overcoming tragedy, into a book packed with lessons that will last a lifetime. His practical formulas will help you map out a plan to lead you from management mess to leadership success."

— **Scott J. Miller**, EVP Thought Leadership @ FranklinCovey, Bestselling Author of *Everyone Deserves A Great Manager* and *Management Mess to Leadership Success*

"John translates his experiences in the cockpit of an F-14 and overcoming life-altering tragedy, into an essential book full of practical formulas for reclaiming the life you've always known you were meant to live."

— **Greg McKeown**, Author of the *New York Times* Bestseller, *Essentialism: The Disciplined Pursuit of Less.*

"I highly recommend reading and implementing *On Purpose with Purpose* in your life. This book helps change the way to think about our past, present and future. Inside of John's intriguing stories and teachings, it is clear that when we deal with the things from our past, that we change the way we think, feel and behave. This new outlook leads to greater success including more influence and happiness with ourselves and others. Thank you and well done, John!"

— **Ford Taylor**, Founder TL/Transformational Leadership/FSH Strategy Consultants Group LLC, Author of *Relational Leadership*

"Without a clear purpose, how will you ever know when you get to where you want to go? Read John Ramstead's book *On Purpose With Purpose* and get a clearer sense of who you are and where you're going. It will make your life more special!"

— **Ken Blanchard**, Coauthor of *The New One Minute Manager*® and *Leading at a Higher Level*

"John Ramstead captures compelling life leadership lessons from his Navy career, his business successes, and his near-death accident, and shows how those experiences helped him become more resilient, more compassionate, and a more effective leader. This book reads more like a novel and is deeply personal, entertaining, and a must read for current and future leaders."

— **Mary C. Kelly**, PhD, Commander, US Navy (ret)

"The best lessons are ones that don't feel like lessons. I was so completely absorbed in John's thrilling stories, relatable examples and thought-provoking exercises. that when I got to the end of the book, I wanted to go back to the beginning and start again. I was respectfully challenged, confidently encouraged, graciously provoked, and tremendously inspired along the way. Highly recommended."

— **Michael Port**, *New York Times* and *Wall Street Journal* Bestselling Author of 8 books including *Steal the Show*

"John Ramstead has an incredibly inspiring story about overcoming real life pain and setbacks. Through it he has become a person of strength and integrity. He is someone you should follow and learn from."

— **Rory Vaden**, *New York Times* Bestselling Author of
Take the Stairs, Cofounder of Brand Builders Group

"As a 27-year Navy SEAL senior leader, I recognize what authentic and effective leadership lessons look like. Rammer's book is the definitive guide to self-determined leadership and provides the essential roadmap to your ultimate destination. A must read!"

— **Steve Drum**, US Navy SEAL Master Chief (Retired),
CEO of Breaching Leadership, LLC

"In his inspiring book, Breaking Through, former F-14 fighter pilot, John Ramstead helps us unlock our potential, live life fully, and become the leaders we were always born to be. From cultivating an abundance mindset while finding passion in work and life, to identifying and moving towards our True North, Breaking Through is a powerful playbook to unlock our leader within both at home and in our careers."

— **Tommy Breedlove**, *Wall Street Journal* and *USA Today*
Bestselling Author of the book *Legendary*

"After 30 years of studying leadership, I've learned to never read a book by an author who calls themselves a Leadership expert or guru. That's what makes John Ramstead different. He calls himself a guide. And that is exactly what he is...the most genuine, authentic and special guide I know. *On Purpose with Purpose* will change your life and also change the lives of those that choose to follow you."

— **Tommy Spaulding**, *New York Times* Bestselling Author of *The
Heart-Led Leader* and *It's Not Just Who You Know*

ON PURPOSE
with PURPOSE

DISCOVERING HOW
TO LIVE YOUR
BEST LIFE

JOHN RAMSTEAD

MOUNT TABOR MEDIA
VERITUM REVELATUM - "TRUTH REVEALED"
A BRANDED IMPRINT OF MORGAN JAMES

NEW YORK

LONDON • NASHVILLE • MELBOURNE • VANCOUVER

ON PURPOSE *with* PURPOSE
DISCOVERING HOW TO
LIVE YOUR BEST LIFE

Published in New York, New York, by Mount Tabor Media, LLC, a branded imprint of Morgan James Publishing. Morgan James is a trademark of Morgan James, LLC. www.MorganJamesPublishing.com

Printed in the United States of America

ISBN 978-1-63195-256-2 paperback
ISBN 978-1-63195-257-9 eBook
Library of Congress Control Number: 2020910402

Cover Design by:
Rachel Lopez
www.r2cdesign.com

*This book is dedicated to my
best friend and wife, Donna, and our three boys.*

CONTENTS

ACKNOWLEDGMENTS

The great glorious masterpiece of man
is to know how to live with purpose.
—Michel de Montaigne

There are so many people who contributed both directly and indirectly to this book. I cannot mention you all, but you know who you are. I am grateful to each and every one of you.

I first want to thank God for saving my life at the accident and giving me a second chance. Thank you for loving me unconditionally and for showing me whom you created me to be and setting me on a path of purpose and conviction.

I'd like to acknowledge my clients and our podcast community who shared their lives with me. Partnering with them as they pursued their dreams and goals has taught me there is always a way forward. I am inspired daily by the power and resilience inside each of us and our infinite capacity for good. A special shout-out to the young team of tomorrow's leaders in Rwanda, who are truly leading a nation and a continent.

Mom and Dad, thank you so much for always being there for me. Mom, you taught me the value of hard work, ingenuity, perseverance, and following one's passions. Dad, I have always counted on you to be my sounding board and to give me valuable advice. You exemplify what it means to be a godly man, and I hope to be just like you when I grow up!

John Harold II, you bless your Mom and me with your kind and generous spirit, your loyalty, and your faithfulness. You have a heart for people, and God works through you on a daily basis. We are so excited to have you and your smart, talented, and fun Kaysey on our team! Michael James, you inspire me with a work ethic that got you from B-level hockey to a state championship team in just a few short years, and I know you will have the same results in your professional life. I am so proud of you and how you have taken to the role of fatherhood. I am not surprised, however, because Mom and I have always cherished your heart of pure gold and love. Matthew Brenner, you amaze me with your unbridled passion for baseball and life, your ability to find humor in every situation, and your crazy-good memory. You bless us all with your love and concern for your family.

My sister, Anne-Marie, and my brother, Nick, thank you for sharing your love for all things literary and your passion for writing and creating. I am so glad some of it rubbed off on me!

My wife's family, Carol, John (who is with Jesus), Denise, James, Mark, and Liz, thank you for making me part of the family from day one and that infamous glass of juice. We love making memories with you. You mean so much to all of us.

All my nieces and nephews, thank you for bringing loads of love and laughter into our world. Watching you grow up and follow your own dreams makes my heart happy.

A heartfelt and special thank-you to the trauma doctors and ICU nurses and Dr. John Van Gilder, my neurosurgeon, at Benefis Hospital in Great Falls, Montana, as well as Dr. Alan Weintraub and the amazing rehab team at Craig Hospital, Denver, without whom I wouldn't be here today. A very special thank-you to Dr. Gary Zuehlsdorff, who was my advocate and went to the mattresses to get me the best care possible through every new medical challenge. You are truly the best.

I am deeply grateful to my writing consultant, Ann Lovett Baird. You taught me how to distill my thinking, blogs, and podcasts into a coherent text. Quite a feat! Thank you for your wisdom and patience as you helped shake my thinking loose to create the message and stories at the heart of this book.

It takes a special friend to stand by you through the ups and downs of writing a book and to actually read that book all the way through multiple times. A special thanks to the consistent encouragement of Steve and Elizabeth Reiter, Jay Cleary, Roy Clark, Keith Boyer, Joe Durnford, Chris McCluskey, Norton Rainey, Ford Taylor, and Cheryl Scanlan. Your support through the long journey will always be meaningful to me. I'm grateful for the reviewers who contributed their feedback, insights, and support: Steve Reiter, Keith Boyer, Jay Cleary, James Webb, Lenwood Ross, Jerry Nichols, John Moyer, Cheryl Scanlan, and Joe Sanders. Steve Reiter, my brother: You were the first one to get to me at my accident and have been with me every step of this amazing journey, including the founding of the Eternal Leadership podcast. I couldn't have done it without you.

To my friend and mentor, Roy Clark, I'll never forget the half day white board session with you that gave me the courage to move to action.

Dawnna St. Louis, the framework for this book was launched at your weekend mastermind retreat. Thank you for always taking time to talk and for setting me on this path. To my coach, Cheryl Scanlan: thank you for your unwavering belief, clarity, and accountability. To my friend Jeff Spadafora: thank you for pouring your life into mine as I walked out this journey. Life is a team sport. Thank you to all of my wingmen at the Halftime Institute and Pinnacle Forum. And thank you to our prayer team at Marketplace Rock—Vicki, Diane, and Amy—for bringing the power of prayer and discernment into this book and our lives.

To my Navy family, the pilots, RIOs, instructors, and skippers who made me better, saved my bacon a time or two, and gave me the best memories and stories a guy could ever ask for: thank you. Special mention for Dan "Darth" Cain and my RIO, Greg "Spike" Hood!

And finally, none of this would have happened without the unfailing support of my wife, Donna. Through the starts and stops, the times when I was stuck, frustrated, and cranky, you encouraged me. You are a true partner. Your insights and advice took this book from good to great. Without you, this book wouldn't be finished. I love you.

FOREWORD

I got to know John, as I participated in his popular podcast and a number of long conversations around the same time. During these conversations, we discovered a lot of alignment of values and philosophies. It was clear to me that John had analytical, personal and organizational thinking. John was prepared for the podcast in a way that obviously was professional and well prepared. Since I do many podcasts—I know the difference. The sessions were planned to be Excellent and John was concerned that our interview would be of benefit and serve the podcast subscribers. That it turned out well was indicative of what he wants to accomplish with his book.

Following the first podcast, it became a treat me for me to converse with John and I was always looking forward to the next conversation and exchange. We even did several more podcasts together.

I consequently was kind of excited when I found that John was writing a book and I was looking forward to reviewing it. I was very intrigued by the title of the book, "On Purpose with Purpose," since Purpose is a subject that I feel very strongly about and consistently discuss in my many speeches and podcasts. It is also an important part of my book, "Excellence Wins."

I received a copy of John's manuscript at an extremely busy time. I was doing a number of Skype podcasts, board meetings, interviews, etc. I simply planned to review the manuscript the following weekend. But at the same time, I took a glance at the first pages and I WAS HOOKED!! Two days later I had not only read it, but had "worked" the whole book.

I am sincerely captured. I feel again very much aligned with the concepts and philosophies. While greatly enjoying the stories around John's life experiences, in the process, I learned more about myself. Now that says a lot since I am 81 years old!

Since I had developed expectations for this book, I was not disappointed! I was drawn in by John's initial experience as a pilot and how it relates to so many moments in each of our lives (although maybe not quite as exciting!) But reading on, I could clearly see how John—as we all are—was very much formed by the experiences of his life! It was very exciting and reading it captured me.

As I "worked" the book, which means I gave myself very sincere personal answers to John's probing questions, it truly served me in my present quest of "finishing well." This is something that will be very different and personal for everyone. But while different, it will be of great value for everyone.

John also shows deeper courage in this book as he is willing to recognize a higher power—GOD! We have to admit—if we are believers or not—that today it takes courage and character to see and openly speak about this higher purpose.

During the reading, I actually felt a deep emotional hope that many will, for their benefit, read this book. Because no doubt, like myself, you will be greatly entertained with great stories and at the same time you will learn about yourself. You will be personally enriched and become a greater leader of yourself and your organization.

As I am finishing to write these few words recognizing John's great work in this book, I am in fact reviewing and "working" it again. I am reviewing "my mindset." I am "gathering intel." I am putting my mindset through the "litmus test." In short—I am improving myself! Thank you, John!

—Horst Schulze

CEO, Horst Schulze Consulting

Chairman Emeritus of Capella Hotel Group

Past President The Ritz Carlton Hotel Company

INTRODUCTION

You want to live a life fully alive.

Leaders—young, old, and in between—share with me all the time that they want to live full lives, work in their strengths, and have meaningful relationships. Their desire goes beyond happiness; they want to know their purpose and feel joy. The problem is they don't know how to get there. It's frustrating. I understand because I've been there too.

You might be standing in a bookstore right now, trying to decide if you should buy a book like this. *On Purpose With Purpose* is about one important truth: *Who* you are—your best self—is the key to unlocking your purpose and your potential. You must take steps to realize and prioritize the worthwhile aspects of your life and have a daily plan for how to move forward. This is how you will create for yourself a life truly and fully alive.

I love stories. In this book, I'll be sharing my favorites to illustrate the principles I believe will propel you forward. There are exciting stories from my F-14 cockpit. There are astounding stories from an accident I should not have survived. There are funny, embarrassing, and sad stories, and some that might challenge you. Each one is here on purpose, for a purpose: to help you move toward the best version of yourself and the truth that, in life, you are the one in control. You need to create a flight plan for your life. In fact, flight planning is so important, I have included a checklist at the end of every chapter for you to work through and share with your wingman! When you understand how to become the best version of yourself, identify a worthwhile goal or dream, and know how to make corrections, that truth will set you free.

Understanding you are the pilot in control of your life is so vital. You have to grab the control stick and throttle with both hands. You also have to identify what might be slowing you down, standing in your way, or stopping you—such as limiting beliefs, mindset, and habits that are not helping you move forward.

Why?

Because it's impossible to go somewhere new, to become someone new, without first acknowledging where you are now. The self-awareness that comes from digging into what you've come to believe about yourself is invaluable. Have you ever felt like you're at the whim of life's circumstances—you're not worthy of an extraordinary life, or you're too busy to make the changes needed to move toward a worthwhile dream or goal? These are all lies we tell ourselves. They come from the world we live in and how we grew up. Our self-talk, social media, TV, movies, and social media reinforce these lies. These lies can be devastating. Because we rarely hear our own voice due to the noise and pressure in the world, we don't take the time to slow down to get to the truth. It might not make sense now but slowing down will accelerate your life.

Early in my career, I was completely driven by the expectations of others. They shaped what and how I lived and worked, as well as why. How I showed up was driven by whom *they* expected me to be, not my authentic self. My definition of success was not my own. I constantly strove to meet a bar as defined by others, but I failed over and over again. I knew only one solution: Work harder and harder. This growing gap between who I was and who I wanted to be led to frustration, burnout, and depression. Every day felt like a marathon I had to complete. On my journey, I have struggled to see myself as an entrepreneur. My marriage has had big ups and downs. I had a low self-image and compensated that with bravado, which hurt relationships along the way.

In this book, I have tried to be totally real about where I have come from, who I am today, and how I got here. Many of us work very hard to maintain a shiny public persona and want to make the hard work look easy from the outside. That the results are effortless is because of our talent and skill. That was how I operated, and it was a lie. When I get to talk to people in person, I always share living life has been the hardest thing I've ever done and also the most rewarding. It's all about finding mentors to figure out how to do the right things the right way at the right time. It's about surrounding yourself with incredible people to encourage, push, and coach you. There are people in my life who have seen more in me than I saw in myself at the time. They believed in me until I believed in myself more. They saw me as someone who was a fighter, who was courageous, who could achieve those big goals in life. In the beginning, when I didn't believe in myself, I had a choice to make. I had to choose to believe what they saw in me. That's what I share with people when they reach out. They can rewrite the script of their lives, make different choices, learn to think differently, and get different results.

My life has not been a straight path by any stretch of the imagination. There have been days when I was frustrated beyond description and angry with myself for failing yet again. As you move forward, there will be days when you feel it is not worth the effort. But here's what I have found: Stick with it. You will find joy on the path to a new destination that will light up your life.

I hope to be a catalyst in the life of others, to equip and inspire them to achieve what they are capable of. This drives everything I do today: letting people know that every day is a second chance for each of us. I get to do this through leadership coaching, speaking, training, and writing. As I have worked with thousands of leaders across North America, Europe, and Africa, my biggest joy is to see each person move forward into life fully alive.

If you're wondering what role faith has in all this, it is extremely important to me. As a Christian, I believe with all my heart that God loves us unconditionally. I was able to experience His full presence and love during and after my accident. That moment changed my life forever. It also gave me the knowledge that all of us are loved deeply, and God uses all circumstances in our lives to work together for good. I see incredible greatness exists in each of us, regardless of our background, experience, or beliefs. Settling for mediocrity is a choice, because if you could see what God sees when He looks at you, the view would knock you alive! There is more to life than you are experiencing now. I share this with everyone I speak to and with everyone who reaches out to me. It might be tough to hear you're more than you've become. The incredible truth is you are completely in control of what you do with that knowledge.

I am not an expert or guru. I see myself more as a Sherpa on Mount Everest. I'm just a few steps ahead of others, and I have been fortunate to learn from others who are a few steps ahead of me. In this book, I share with you exactly what I have learned along the way: how I was able to pick up the pieces and reassemble them in a way that created a whole new life—a life I could only dream about as I lay in bed at night staring at the ceiling.

Hope is a powerful force in the world; hope that tomorrow can be better than today, and next year can be better than last year. My goal is to give you hope, show you a path forward, and help you create a personal action plan so, each day, you know exactly what you need to do to live a life fully alive, a life *on* purpose, *with* purpose.

I believe in you,

John

THE DREAM

I t's February 1991. My RIO (Radar Intercept Officer) and I are strapped into the ejection seats of our F-14 Tomcat, on the flight deck of the aircraft carrier USS *Independence* in the Persian Gulf, ready for our first combat mission. My stomach is churning as the flight deck crew slowly taxis my F-14 forward. They lock it into the number four steam-powered catapult, which holds the aircraft securely in place until we are launched into the air. I ease the throttle forward to go to full power while the check crew is busy with their final inspection. With a thumbs-up from the lead petty officer, the launch officer then gives me the signal to push the throttles forward beyond full power to full afterburner. My jet is now burning 2,000 pounds of fuel per minute, and we are vibrating with energy and anticipation. After making sure everything is good to go on my instrument panel, the last item on my checklist is to salute the launch officer.

Just before I raise my arm, I have one overwhelming feeling: *Don't launch!* All my flight training, practice, and flight competitions with other naval aviators is going to be tested right here, right now, and I'm not sure I'm ready. Then, BOOM! We go from 0 to 150 mph in 2.4 seconds, and there is no time for doubt. I claw my way off the deck and into the sky to form up with my wingman. All of the knowledge, training, and desire to accomplish our mission with excellence is kicking in, along with a hefty dose of adrenaline.

I know whoever sees the enemy first typically wins. My conditioned response is laser-like focus in this kill-or-be-killed situation. In this environment, I have to make decisions early and often, and I don't have the luxury to second-guess myself.

Looking Back

That day, I discovered I was capable of more than I thought I was, thanks to the impact and influence of incredible men and women in my life. These were people who saw more in me than I saw in myself. Their support pushed me forward to a stronger belief in what was possible for me.

In my years as a naval aviator, call sign "Rammer," I had to have an attitude of humility to survive. What I was doing required split-second decisions, such as precise maneuvering of a 72,000-pound gorilla at up to 1,195 miles per hour. I always had incredible respect for the team and the powerful craft I was piloting. The combat controller on the ground was giving the location of both friendly and enemy aircraft I needed to spot or call "no joy," which was our slang for: *I don't have a visual on the bogey.* A *bogey* is an aircraft I can see but cannot yet identify as hostile or friendly. My backseater, or RIO, was giving invaluable support as we worked as a team. My wingman, flying one mile to my right and slightly behind in combat spread, completed the formidable formation that allowed us to react to what was around us. Since I was the lead, he would follow my direction. If the attack shifted to the wingman, then our roles could instantly shift, which took clear communication and years of practice.

Landing an F-14 on an aircraft carrier was like touching down on a postage stamp in the middle of a vast sea. There were days we saw waves that were 30 feet high, with wind gusts of 50 miles per hour, and the flight deck was pitching and rolling like a bad carnival ride. I had to trust my instruments, training, and crew completely. On a perfect approach, as I crossed the ramp at the back of the ship to put my tailhook into the wires, I had only 12 feet of clearance between me and the hard steel of the flight deck. Everyone on the carrier had to be totally aware every second of where they were and of what was happening around them. Being in the wrong place at the wrong time could be deadly.

Landing the F-14 on the carrier always stirred mixed emotions for me. My heart would race in my chest, the blood would pound in my ears, and my throat would tighten as my comfort zone was constantly stretched. This was especially true during night landings, which never got comfortable for me or any aviator I knew. At the same time, I felt sheer exhilaration and pure joy commanding this awesome machine through boundless skies, executing our mission to protect and serve our country and conquer our foes. Every decision I made had significant consequences. This was when I learned to *fail forward*, or use what didn't go right to improve the next time. There were times filled with extreme confidence that could quickly turn to self-doubt. It was a place where I felt fully alive! Every day was a new experience and a step closer to a worthwhile goal and dream.

Then, my biggest dream came true. I was assigned to Top Gun, the most prestigious group of pilots in the Navy. This is what I had dreamed of for so many years. All the training, the work, and the harrowing experiences were about to pay off in spades. On a sunny Sunday afternoon, the dream was ripped from my grasp. I was pitching a squadron softball practice when a line drive hit my right eye and fractured the bones around it. I was no longer able to fly. The Navy invited me to retire. With my dream in pieces, I had no idea where I would land.

Fast-forward to 2011. Retired from the military, I was at the top of my game professionally. As an entrepreneur, I experienced some significant highs and lows. I had started two nonprofits and was on a number of boards. My wife and I had been married for twenty-two years, and we had three amazing boys. Sounds great, right? Here's the "but," and it was huge for me: I couldn't get past the broken heart I suffered on that softball field. I was no longer part of an elite team of fighter pilots flying Mach 2 in an F-14 jet, risking my life every time I sat in the cockpit. I was no longer striving toward a huge dream while being on a mission I loved with every fiber of my being, serving and protecting this amazing country and the inspiring people who make it great. I felt lost, like my life had drifted permanently off course.

Airplanes do get off course. Think about the last time you were in a commercial airliner, sitting comfortably at altitude as the jet cruised along. What percentage of the time do you think the airplane is on course when the crew has the autopilot engaged? Would you like to think it's on course 100 percent of the time? Maybe you're a little more skeptical and would guess it's on course about 50 percent of the time. What if I told you the plane on which you are flying is on course *less than 3 percent of the time?* The pilot must intentionally and repeatedly bring the plane back on course so it arrives at its destination.

Life is like a jet flying to its destination. From the time your wheels leave the runway, you are off course at least 97 percent of the time. You are the one in control—period. To reach your destination of optimal health, significance, prosperity, or creating a legacy, you must do what a pilot does.

You need three things to arrive at your destination without running out of gas or crashing and burning on the way:

You must have a navigational reference, *True North*.

You must determine your *Destination*.

You must accurately determine your *Present Position*.

I had lost track of all three of these things in my life. I had drifted to a place I didn't even know how to describe. When my coach, Jeff Spadafora, called it "smoldering discontent," it was a light-bulb moment.

I said to him, "That's exactly how I feel!"

Smoldering discontent had grown little by little in my heart and mind. I didn't get off course in an instant. Small choices and decisions I made every day ended up taking me to a place in my life where I didn't really want to be.

I was working up to eighty hours a week to support my family. My relationships with my sons and my wife had deteriorated. This was supposed to be *it*. According to the world, I had *made it*, yet I was miserable. My discontent led me to feel isolated. Many days, I didn't even feel like going home because I had created a negative environment that was impacting my whole family.

At this time, Dr. James Dobson invited me to a retreat at a beautiful ranch in Great Falls, Montana. The skies were blue, dotted with a few puffy clouds. It was 55° with a slight breeze that smelled like the alpine mountains surrounding us. We arrived on Thursday afternoon, and the plan was to ride horses to a plateau on the property for lunch on Friday. I was the first one saddled and was ready for a docile trail ride.

My horse started out at a trot, then made a sharp 90-degree turn to the right and started galloping. I was thrown back, so the horse's rump was battering my shoulder blades. I did the only thing I knew to keep from falling off the horse. I squeezed my legs around his middle. Little did I know that I was signaling the horse to go faster. As I was able to pull myself back up, I started pulling on the reins. He wouldn't turn or slow down. Overwhelming panic and fear washed over me as we approached a steel corral fence. I had flown in combat and was raising teenage boys, but nothing had prepared me for this. Have you ever had a moment when time slowed down, and you had perfect clarity? When I was thirty yards from the fence at a full gallop, with the sound of hooves thundering in my ears, I remember thinking very clearly: *This is not going to end well!* Then, it was lights out.

My head and chest slammed into the fence. My face was crushed, neck broken, ribs broken, and my lung punctured. When I came to on the ground, the pain was excruciating. I was screaming and I could hear people praying for me. Later, one of the people who was standing there told me that I became very calm, and it was as though I was sinking into the ground. At that moment, I experienced the presence of God surrounding me. I was overwhelmed with the feeling of God's love and acceptance. I had the feeling that no matter what I did or didn't do in the past, I was totally accepted by Him. As God's presence surrounded me, He told me that He was not ready to take me home to heaven, so I knew that I was not going to die. I knew He had plans for me beyond what I had accomplished so far.

After an hourlong wait, I was life-flighted to Benefis Hospital Trauma Center, where I spent four weeks in the ICU and another week on a step-down floor. During that time, I was in and out of surgeries for a severe traumatic brain injury and multiple other injuries. Due to the seriousness of my condition, I have few recollections of what was going on right after the accident. According to multiple doctors, my accident wasn't survivable, and they were amazed that I wasn't a quadriplegic like the actor Christopher Reeve. I will never forget the day that a well-meaning doctor told Donna and me that I would probably not even be able to be the greeter at a big box store. Everyone told me I had to come to grips with my new normal. But because God had told me that He was going to heal me, I was confident that my new normal would be the same as the old normal. That was not the case. He didn't heal me the way I was expecting Him to.

There were days when I thought I would never again be able to be a good husband or father. I feared that I wouldn't be able to provide for my family. I thought of the success I had in business and realized those days might be over forever.

The pain I experienced was never-ending and overwhelming. I was allowed pain meds only once every four hours. For about the first thirty minutes, they relieved my pain. When I had an hour left until I could have the next dose of pain medicine, I would watch the clock and break down the hour into five-minute increments. I focused on surviving the pain for five minutes. When I did that, I felt I had a victory. Then, I focused on the next five minutes, and the next. That's the only way I was able to make it through that horribly painful last hour until I could get another thirty minutes of relief.

My recovery took more than two years, twenty-three surgeries, and twenty months of rehabilitation at Craig Hospital, a state-of-the-art hospital in Denver for people suffering from brain and spinal cord injuries. It was a time of amazing growth in which I learned to fight to survive. I had to fight through constant recoveries from surgery and tough rehabilitation.

The reason I was able to continue to fight through all the pain and recovery was that extraordinary encounter with God at the accident scene. That changed everything.

God didn't tell me exactly what to do; He told me who to be.

He gave me a mission unlike the missions I had as a pilot. This mission would never be totally achieved. There's no ending to it because it drives everything I do to this day.

Though from the outside the accident might have looked like a tragedy, God used it to bring me to my life's purpose. Having to dig deep into my true identity as I did after the accident resulted in living my life more fully than I ever have. But it's more than that; I want others to do the same. I am passionate about providing people with the tools they need to create an extraordinary life and get the results they want. I want to help people live their dreams, to find the disciplines they need to follow their God-given mission in life. I want people to know that even the situations and events in their lives that aren't pretty or pleasant *will* work together for good. My experiences and passions have led me to become an executive and leadership coach. Every day, I live my life's purpose and employ my passions to help others.

I believe that self-knowledge is key to building fine leaders. Leadership teaching and training is a huge industry. If you search the term on *Amazon,* over 30,000 titles come up. After reading hundreds of leadership books, being mentored, and applying what I have learned, I have come to one definitive observation: The leadership industry is broken. The primary focus of most leadership training is on figuring out the why, what, and how. I can take the best teachings of someone else and apply them, but I will not get a fraction of their results. This is because of the one thing that the leadership industry ignores that is essential: *who* you are. In this book, you will learn the small steps it will take to enable you to become your very best version of yourself.

During my recovery time, I had another key revelation. Prior to the accident, I had been trying to fly solo, which is something we would *never* do as pilots. As a fighter pilot, I *always* had a wingman. I realized that I needed others to help me through life's journey.

As pilots, we lived by the checklist. We had checklists for everything you can imagine. In this book, we'll employ the checklist and the wingman concepts to help you create your own Flight Plan. At the end of every chapter in this book, you will find a checklist to be completed with your own wingman or accountability partner. My hope is that you will use everything you learn in this book to create the life you want and achieve all that you want to achieve. Then, if it's meaningful to you, share it with others who will benefit from it and become a wingman for someone else. Leadership is having a positive influence on at least one other person. When you help others become the best version of themselves and reach their full potential, they can do that for others in their sphere of influence. That is how you live a life beyond influence.

In the following chapters, we will look at your True North, Destination, and Present Position—the three things a pilot needs to know for any flight. These can be applied to your life, too, and we will explore how they apply to you throughout the book.

I hope that you will find yourself breaking through the clouds to your own fulfilling life of clarity and purpose, always pointing toward your True North and moving toward your life's Destination.

TRUE NORTH

If you could go anywhere, where would you like to go? Not in terms of vacations, but in your life. You see, we're all on a journey, whether we know it or not. We are traveling inevitably toward the ends of our lives. So, the real question for us is whether we're going to select a destination and steer a course for it or allow ourselves to be swept along with the tide, letting others determine where we'll end up. The choice is entirely up to us.
—John C. Maxwell

A s I mentioned earlier, the three things a pilot must know at all times during any flight are True North, Destination, and Present Position. As a pilot, being clear about the direction in which you are going is a life-or-death situation. In the cockpit, and in life, knowing True North is fundamental to successful navigation.

My RIO and I had a harrowing experience of losing our True North. Our combat mission in Iraq was complete. I climbed out southward toward Mother, which was our affectionate name for the aircraft carrier USS *Independence*. She was floating far away. I had to climb to 43,000 feet, where the engines were most fuel efficient, in order to have enough fuel to make it. Once I reached that altitude, the adrenalin subsided, and I turned off my cockpit lights to enjoy the view. Not one light was visible on the ground, but above us, the sight was unbelievable. The stars and galaxies were so bright that I did not need cockpit lights to read my instruments. I was sure only God could have created something like this. I was having an amazing moment, lost in the splendor of the heavens.

My RIO ruined the moment, his voice piercing the beauty. "Rammer, our INS is down, and I can't get a lock on our recovery coordinates."

That meant we didn't know exactly where the aircraft carrier was. That night we were operating EMCON, which stands for *emission control*. Due to threats in the area, the aircraft carrier wasn't transmitting anything—zip, nada. No radar, radio, or navigational signals. It was my least favorite recovery, especially since it was at night. It was our responsibility to self-navigate back to the boat for night recovery operations. The coordinates of the boat had been shared during our mission brief, but now we were out over the Persian Gulf with no compass to tell us True North. F-14 instrument panels do not have a traditional compass. Everything is shown on our navigation displays. The steering vectors are driven by the INS. Since the system didn't know where we were, the directions to the next waypoint were meaningless. We had been briefed on EMCON recovery, which, to be effective, requires complete radio silence by all aircraft.

As a last resort, my RIO could have radioed, "Redcrown, this is Oak 27 transmitting in the blind. We are squawking 1137 and need a vector to Mother, how copy?" We would have endangered many lives and failed our mission.

Honestly, I was more worried about failing in our mission and the negative consequences for my RIO and me than about anything else at that moment. If we had made that radio call, the carrier would have been at risk, and the consequences to us professionally could have been severe. If we had guessed wrong and run out of gas, we would have had to eject over the Persian Gulf. Not only would we have been in a dangerous open-water survival situation, but the Gulf is filled with fifty-seven varieties of deadly sea snakes. If we had been bitten by one, the only way for the flight surgeons to administer the correct antivenin would have been to catch and identify the snake that had bitten us…*Right.*

Somehow, we made a couple of educated guesses and found Mother. We saw other aircraft lights as they landed on the USS *Independence.* Then, we could navigate safely to Mother. How we managed to figure out where we were and how to get home is truly a miracle.

In life and business, your True North is your guiding light—a way to keep you on track with your vision, your purpose, your why. Knowing your personal True North is the first step in creating an extraordinary life. Your True North will always give you a gauge for course correction in your life. It's easy to veer slowly off track. If you don't know what your True North is, how will you know how to course-correct?

My faith houses my True North. Thinking about what God would do in a situation guides what I do. What He has modeled for me is to trust Him through all of life's ups and downs. Each of us has a unique purpose we are perfectly prepared for. A core value for me is to love others unconditionally, which means I strive to see the best in others, not judge people who make mistakes, and help them move in the right direction. We all have flaws and make mistakes every day, but what a world this would be if we all helped each other up instead of kicking those who are down.

True North will keep you on track in spite of ambiguity and change in your life. Sometimes, what you are actually doing may shift from season to season in your life, but your True North will keep you in check.

The second critical factor in a successful flight is knowing your Destination. This requires clear, specific long-term, short-term, and mid-range goals, written down, including daily steps to accomplish them. Next, you launch toward that Destination with no guarantee of success. You must be willing to move out of your comfort zone and take risks, even though you know most of what you attempt will not succeed, at least not in the beginning.

The third part is the real secret of success. Prepare to make continual Course Corrections. Just as an aircraft faces headwinds, downdrafts, storm fronts, wind shear, lightning, and unexpected turbulence, you will experience challenges in the pursuit of any worthwhile goal.

To achieve success and significance, keep your mind fixed clearly on your Destination, yet remain flexible about how you achieve your goals. Be open to new input and ideas. Learn from every experience. Look for the lesson in every setback or difficulty.

And here is the most important secret to success of all: You must resolve in advance that you will *never* give up. Your ability to persist in the direction of your goal in the face of all adversity is what will ultimately guarantee your success.

And here is the most important secret to success of all: You must resolve in advance that you will *never* give up.

You make your own "luck" through your own hard work and determination. Decide upon your Destination, take off, and be open to making continual Course Corrections until you reach your goal.

So, how can you determine your own True North?

True North in your life is based on three things:

- Identity
- Values
- Mindset

Sometimes getting back to True North will take some intuition, in the way that my RIO and I found our way back to the aircraft carrier. Instruments in the cockpit are key to navigation, but in the example of when we were over the Persian Gulf, the instruments were of little help. When you don't have external instruments to show you the way, it's time to determine your internal navigational instruments that show you True North and guide you home.

Time and time again, *Identity* is the part of leadership development that is often missing for those who struggle to find their True North. As difficult as it was to endure, my accident actually brought me to a deeper sense of my own identity.

Your values are the underpinning of your identity, and they drive your actions. They represent your unique and individual essence. You must have a clear picture of what your values are and their importance in your life.

Last but not least, you have to master your mindset. Your mindset is the lens through which you see the world and process what is happening in your world. Do you see yourself as a victor or a victim? Do you tend to react from a place of judgment or do you seek to learn and understand?

Our lives are dynamic. When something happens in our world, our mindset informs how we feel and how we act. Repeated actions over time become habits. Ask yourself, does your mindset and the actions you choose to take in a given situation move you toward or away from a life fully alive? If you feel like the results you are currently getting in life could be better, then mastering and changing your mindset is the first step.

In the chapters that follow, we dive into these three areas in greater detail and discuss how to incorporate them into your life.

Identity

> *No matter how hard you try, you cannot consistently behave*
> *in a way that is inconsistent with how you see yourself.*
> **—Zig Ziglar**

How do you view yourself? At a point early in my military career, others saw more in me than I saw in myself. Later in life, as I recovered from my accident, I had to fight for my new and true identity. In the long term, understanding and engaging in my true identity is the lynchpin of my fulfilled life. Prior to my accident, I felt like I could outwork everyone else. And yet, I ended up in a place of smoldering discontent, drifting without direction and feeling like I wasn't making any progress.

Have you ever felt like your life is an endless workout on a treadmill, as you try your hardest, dripping sweat but getting nowhere? Does that little voice keep telling you you're not good enough, the last success you achieved is a fluke and won't last? You are running on fumes and don't even realize it. Every Sunday night, you have to steel yourself for the week and make the commitment to get to Friday. You resign yourself to the work ahead, with the frustration in the back of your mind that you'll never get off this treadmill. You find yourself stuck in this place because you have not connected with your true identity.

My Personal Identity Journey

It was a bright fall day in October of 1989, and I was sitting in the ready room for Training Squadron 19 at Naval Air Station in Meridian,

Mississippi. We were playing cards, waiting for our training flight briefing to start. All of a sudden, we heard people shouting. People were running down the passageways, and there was a commotion at the duty desk. We all ran to see what happened.

"There was a mishap on the Lex!"

The Lex was the USS *Lexington*, a Korean War-era aircraft carrier we now used for training. One of the most significant rites of passage of a Navy jet pilot student aviator is the first time they land on an aircraft carrier.

Earlier that morning, I had talked with my good friend Steve, who was in the intermediate jet training class ahead of me. He was getting ready to head to the flight line and join his class, flying to the Lex for their first attempt at carrier landings.

Steve was one of the good guys. He was quick with a smile when he knew you were stressed, always encouraging others and freely sharing what he learned in training situations to help those around him get better.

Before we are allowed to go to the ship for the first time, every student had to practice hundreds of field carrier landings, which simulated landing on an aircraft carrier at sea. Once students passed the field qualifications, they were signed off by those in command to head out to the boat to try their first landings at sea.

When he attempted his first landing, Steve came in at the wrong angle. Instead of approaching the landing deck lined up with the centerline and on the glide slope (correct angle of approach), he had rolled out behind the boat to the right of the landing deck centerline and above the glide slope. As he tried to correct, his jet ended up slow and underpowered. Slowing down below the optimal landing speed while landing on an aircraft carrier can create an unrecoverable situation, even at full thrust.

The Landing Signal Officer (LSO) stationed on the back of the boat hit the wave-off button that set red lights flashing all over the deck and was yelling, "Power! Power! Power!" into the radio, warning Steve to abort the landing and climb back to a safe altitude.

As Steve attempted to do this, his nose pitched up, and he lost control of the aircraft as it entered an approach turn stall. This flipped him upside down. The T-2C slammed into the ship's superstructure, cartwheeling onto the deck in a fiery explosion. As the plane crashed into the deck in a ball of smoke and fire, Steve and four other crewmembers died, and nineteen others were injured.

The Navy required us to review the video of the accident in what is called a *safety stand-down*, in an effort to prevent similar future mishaps. I watched in horror: The plane slammed into the boat, and firefighting crews frantically extinguished the flames from the burning jet fuel produced in the crash.

One week later, as I walked outside the chapel at Naval Air Station Meridian, Mississippi, for Steve's funeral, I was holding it together pretty well. I looked up into the sky; four T-2C Buckeye jet trainers were roaring toward us. The third plane in the formation pulled straight up toward heaven, just as they approached the chapel. It's what the Navy calls the *missing man formation*. At that moment, I broke down in tears at the finality of Steve's death, as well as the knowledge that three weeks from then, I was going to be lining up behind the USS *Lexington* for my first attempt to land on the aircraft carrier. I questioned everything about what I was doing, why I was doing it, and the cost it might extract. Never before had I been required to search my soul and truly connect with my personal *why*. I had to come to grips with my true identity. My gut reaction was: *I can't give up on my dream.* My second thought was: *If I keep moving forward, it might cost me my life.* I couldn't just head back down to the flight line, put on my gear, and jump in the cockpit for the next training mission. It was time for some deep soul-searching.

I called my fiancée. I called my father. I spoke with trusted mentors who were my instructors in the squadron. I was in a place of severe identity crisis. Did I have what it takes to become a Navy fighter pilot, flying off aircraft carriers, or was that a silly dream, utterly out of my reach, that I had been pursuing out of vanity?

I had to slow down to reflect on why I had chosen this path. I examined my skills to assess what I was good at. I made the conscious choice to accept I had the ability to succeed in one of the most demanding environments in existence. It turned out the decision I made that day was a pivotal point in my life.

When I chose with absolute certainty I would continue Navy flight training, I started to see myself differently. I saw myself as someone who could achieve great things, whose life could have worth. I embraced the truth that if I followed my dreams, I could save lives and add value to the lives of our men and women in uniform.

Sometimes it takes an extraordinary event for us to come face-to-face with our true nature. We must lean into that true identity if we are to move forward. If we believe the lie of a false identity we've accepted, it will prevent us from achieving our highest potential.

Why Finding Your True Identity Is Vital

As you can see, my soul-searching experience—even though it came out of an event so tragic—caused me to doubt pursuing my dream. The result was pivotal. It changed the way I viewed myself.

This is why your identity, based on your authentic self, is so important. If you let others define your identity, you could miss what you are meant to do on Earth. You could end up on that treadmill until your deathbed. Knowing exactly who you are will enable you to continue toward your True North. In addition, if you don't operate from your true self, people will suspect you are a counterfeit, which will seriously damage your personal and business relationships.

Gathering Intel—Consider These Questions

If you could wave a magic wand, what would you share if we got together for coffee a year from now?

What dream would you love to accomplish?

Have there been significant life events that caused you to give up on your dream or hold it tighter? Why?

Have your fears slowed you down or stood in your way?

Have you been feeling a smoldering discontent?

Let's keep the answers to these questions in mind as we explore your true identity.

Your True Identity

So, what is your identity, anyway? Your True Identity is your authentic self. It is how you are wired. Remember when you were a child and anything was possible? As your authentic self, you surrender the labels and titles others have given you. Your identity is more than who you are now. It is also what you can do and who you can become. It is freedom, joy, and possibility.

Your identity is formed throughout your life. It comes from the sum total of all of your experiences, both your successes and failures. It comes from what others have said to you and what you think other people think about you. You may have accepted as truths lies about who you are. I believe these chains of a falsely accepted identity hold you back from living life fully alive.

It is time to break the chains!

Constructed Versus True Self

The level of stress and discontent you feel is directly related to the gap between the person you see in the mirror and the version of you that is true—your best self. The bigger the gap between your constructed and authentic self, the more stress you will feel. You will spend a lot more energy trying to live up to someone who isn't you at the core. This can make you physically sick. At some point, to get from your falsely constructed identity to your true, authentic identity, you have to shift from limiting beliefs to liberating truths. This shift requires self-discovery and work.

Working on your authentic self requires you to look honestly at yourself and determine where you need to make shifts in behavior in order to act like your true self. You might need to adjust the thermostat. A thermostat is designed to keep the status quo regarding the temperature in your home. You have to set the thermostat to a higher or lower temperature to get a different result in the room. Your internal behavior thermostat does the same thing. You have to be willing to give up the status quo in life to get a different result.

My identity has been formed from fifty-three years of living. After my accident, I had to rethink my identity. When I started this work, I was so close to the issues that it was a huge challenge for me to discern the facts from fiction. To make meaningful progress, I needed help to get to the core of my authentic self and move toward that person. I needed a coach to help.

A good coach or mentor will help you reflect, and they will guide you to your most authentic self. The experience of working with an amazing coach was so transformational, I decided to become an executive and leadership coach myself.

One of my clients had a shift in his mindset based on the work we did with his true identity. He had a dream—to start a company in the industry he knew well. He determined his company would do business differently. The company would enrich the lives of employees, clients, and partners. This business would have a positive impact on the city where he lived.

People my client respected had told him he would never succeed as an entrepreneur, and that, if he left his corporate job, he would be putting his family, finances, and career at risk. He had accepted as truth what people said of his identity. As the years went by, he drifted into a place of smoldering discontent in every area of his life. He told me he wanted to feel alive but had no idea what that looked like or how to get there. His limiting beliefs kept him trapped in the vision of becoming a CEO and held back by the fear of failing if he did become a CEO.

The opposite side of a limiting belief is a liberating truth. As we worked together to clarify who he was at the core—his strengths, gifts, passions, and values—a picture of his true identity emerged. He realized the truth of *who* he was; he was actually wired to be a *successful* entrepreneur and CEO. Imagine a race car with the throttle floored, the wheels spinning, and the smoke from the burnt rubber filling the air, but the car isn't moving. That is because the parking brake is on. This shift was like dropping the parking brake, and he was off to the races.

Instead of my client going to war with a corporate situation, he embraced the truth of who he is at the core. No matter what everyone around him said, he chose to focus on his own truth about himself. Ultimately, his results as an entrepreneur far exceeded what he could have accomplished by accepting others' views and perceptions of him. Today, the company he founded is thriving, he has an incredible team, and he will tell you he is living life fully alive!

Your true identity is not some buried treasure you can discover all at once. Finding it is a process that evolves over time. As you become aware of the truth and lies of your current self, the authentic self will emerge. Stepping into your true identity will allow you to realize your life purpose and live it. The opinions of others will slowly fade to background noise.

One of the most important questions
you can ask is: Who am I really?

As Howard Thurman, noted African American author and civil rights leader, said, "Don't ask yourself what the world needs. Ask yourself, 'What makes me come alive?' and go do it. Because what the world needs is [men and women] who have come alive."

This is a personal journey we all need to take. My friend Lloyd Reeb is a coach for the Halftime Institute and has coached thousands of leaders through this process. I asked him to describe the key factor in connecting to our true identity.

He said, "That is simple—slow down."

We live in a hyper-caffeinated, Mach 5 world, and slowing down is the last thing we make time for; yet, that is what it will take. Finding your true identity is a process of rooting out the lies and shedding layers that don't serve you well in creating the life you were meant to live.

Once you slow down and root out the lies, then you can take the next small step forward into embracing your purpose and unique destiny. Recognize your individual greatness, and at the same time, acknowledge your past experiences and the adversity you have dealt with. Approach this journey with intense curiosity rather than judgment. Give yourself a break from your inner voice and the critical voice of others.

I've found that critics in my life aren't even thinking about me and honestly don't care if I stay stuck in smoldering discontent or step into a life fully alive. Critics keep you trapped in your false identity and locked in your box. So, ignore them! With these principles in mind, let's look at an identity process that works.

Before we dive in, consider these questions:

Think back to your childhood when anything was possible and labels hadn't yet defined you. What did you dream of doing?

_____

_____

Who did you dream of becoming?

_____

_____

Is it possible you have accepted lies about yourself? What might they be?

_____

_____

What limiting beliefs do you have about yourself?

_____

_____

_____

Is there someone in your life who can be completely honest with you about these questions? If not, can you think of someone you could ask to be your wingman or mentor?

_____

_____

_____

True Identity

Let's look at a process of creating clarity that I think every one of us needs. It's something my clients seek. People who are in career transition, entrepreneurs running companies, people faced with major life decisions, or those who are ready for more meaningful lives come to me with the same question: *What is my higher purpose?*

Cross-Section of Your Personal Assets and Your Passion

Living according to your true identity or purpose means you will find the cross-section of your personal assets, talents, skills, experiences, and your passion. So, it's a matter of using your unique gifts, talents, and skills and following your passions. Before we dive into the details, here's a graph to give you some context.

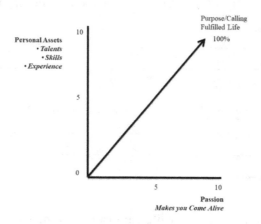

Intersection of Personal Assets and Passions

On the horizontal axis across the bottom, you can rate how well you are living your passion from 1 to 10. On the vertical axis on the left, you can rate how well you are using your gifts, talents, and skills on a scale of 1 to 10. Your goal is to move toward the upper right-hand corner to a 10 out of 10, in which you are living life according to your true identity. In this example, we can see that if you rate a 7 out of 10 on gifts, talents, and skills, but only 3 for passions, the score of 7 times 3 means you are operating at 21 percent of your full potential or true identity. So, even though you are at 7 for gifts, talents, and skills, because you are only operating at 3 out of 10 on passion, you have an overall rating of only 21 percent.

Let's say you are a talented, skilled, and gifted teacher. In terms of fulfillment, when you are teaching, you are fully engaged in your talents, so you have a 10 score, but if you are teaching a subject that you are not passionate about, you might be at a level 3 for passion. That is only 30 percent, and you are leaving 70 percent on the table.

So, it makes sense that you want to be living at a level 10 out of 10. That means you want a level 10 in terms of what you're gifted in doing, merging with a level 10 on what brings you the most alive—your passion. And I promise you when you're at a level 10 out of 10, you're doing the thing you were created to do.

When I worked on Wall Street, I rated a 9 out of 10 in my gifts but a 3 out of 10 in my passion. Think about that for a second. 3 x 9 = 27. That means in terms of a 10-out-of-10 life, I was only 27 percent of the way there. Is it any wonder I felt so frustrated? My destiny and potential were left 73 percent unfulfilled.

Let's take a deeper look at your gifts, talents, skills, and how to find your passion.

Inventory Your Personal Assets

1) Identify Your Talents.

Talents are what you are naturally good at, those things you have always had an aptitude for. What are your talents? What are the things you do naturally? If you are good at something but don't like doing it, then don't include it in your inventory. What do you like to do but think you don't do well? What do people compliment you on? Perhaps you have even dismissed or rejected their affirmations, but include them in this list for now.

What are your talents?

_____

_____

_____

_____

_____

2) Determine Skills to Support Your Purpose.

A *skill* is something that you have learned and practiced. A skill can also be an area of expertise. Inventory your skills to see which ones will support your purpose and determine additional skills that you need to learn to accomplish your purpose.

For example, perhaps your purpose is to help people retire comfortably, and you've decided that you need to move into advising people on investing; or you have been in the banking business, and you decide to become a stockbroker. Skills you probably possess are communicating with customers, analyzing the customers' businesses to see what kind of loans they might need, or bundling products to save them money. Licensure may be required to assure others you have achieved a level of skill or competency; for instance, to become a stockbroker, you must acquire certain licenses in order to legally advise customers regarding stock choices and investment strategies.

You possess other skills that may not support your purpose. For example, you may have learned to be a great gardener, but that's not a skill that impacts your ultimate purpose in life in this case.

If you have ever taken a personality profile, like Meyers-Briggs, DISC, or Strength Finders, that is a great resource to refer to as you take inventory.

What are your skills?

_____

_____

_____

_____

_____

3) Identify Experiences That Support Your Purpose.

All your work and life experiences can play into your purpose. Perhaps you decide that your purpose is to facilitate families managing their family businesses in a way that's equitable to all and keeps family relationships intact. In this scenario, you might have experience as a commercial banker that serves that purpose. You might also have experience in advising people in relationship dynamics or personal experience running a family-owned business. All these experiences work together to support your purpose.

What experiences support your purpose?

_____

_____

_____

_____

_____

Find Your Passion

It took a life-changing event for me to discover the power of passions. If I had not gone through my accident—desperate to find meaning and purpose, as well as a way to earn a living—who knows how much longer it would have taken for me to discover my passions. Looking back, I feel very fortunate to have figured them out. Without the beautiful pursuits that my search uncovered, my life and business would be very different. Perhaps I would have lived my whole life in a place of smoldering discontent.

Doing what you love to do has a fantastic impact in every area of your life. It's like the line from one of my favorite movies, *Gladiator* (Universal Pictures and Dreamworks Pictures, 2000) when, just before battle, Maximus proclaims, "Brothers, what we do in life echoes in eternity."

I believe you are created for greatness. Every time you cross the pathway of your passion, you come alive. Your passion connects your heart to your destiny as you walk the journey of life. Currently, you are probably weaving in and out of moments of living your passion. Your goal is to get to a place in which you recognize the moments when you are 100 percent fully alive and are experiencing them often.

Your Passion Search—How to Find Your Passion

1) Identify What You Love to Do

Whatever you absolutely love to do will help clue you in to what your passion is. When you talk about something in a way that lights up your heart, face, and voice, that's a passion.

Here's an example. I was working with a client and asked him, "What are you passionate about?"

The first thing out of his mouth was "Fly fishing!"

"That's great," I said. "What about fly fishing are you are passionate about?"

"It's the time alone in nature, with the sound of the river running, when I feel closest to God, and we talk."

I asked, "So, would it be fair to say that you are passionate about being alone in nature and communing with God?"

"Yes!" he said.

"What else about fly fishing brings you alive?"

"I love volunteering as a fly-fishing guide for Healing Waters, which is a nonprofit that takes wounded veterans into the mountains and teaches them how to fly fish. I love spending the day with these incredible warriors. When they catch their first fish, we take a picture next to the river with them holding the trout they just caught before we release it. Everyone has huge smiles, and I can see their joy."

"It sounds like you are passionate about teaching people a valuable new skill and seeing them succeed in it," I said.

He came alive. "Yes! I love mentoring people in my company, seeing them succeed, and working with veterans, as well as with my son."

In that moment, my client realized that his biggest passions are equipping people with what they need to succeed, to engage in meaningful conversations, and spend more time in solitude to recharge his battery and talk with God. He applied these discoveries and changed everything he was doing as the CEO of his 300-person company. He transitioned from being the decision-maker to equipping everyone around him to make better decisions and lead more effectively. As a result, the company started growing again, and he went from being frustrated and burned out to being alive and moving toward a 10-out-of-10 life!

Learning what you love to do and what you are good at is one of the quickest ways to identify the passions in your life. If what you love doesn't seem practical or common, write it down anyway. It could be a bigger clue than you realize. You don't need to be good at something for it to qualify as a passion. It might not generate income either. When it comes to finding your passions, your talents are clues. What matters most is whether you feel energized when you think about these passions.

2) Pay Attention to What and Who Bothers You

What do people around you do that is annoying? Examine what makes those things annoying. For example, gossip and negative talk annoy me. I have come to discover the real reason for this is I'm passionate about having meaningful conversations about what truly matters in others' lives.

I had spent my life being an overachieving, striving-to-meet-expectations-of-others businessman. When I embarked on this adventure after my accident, I had to give myself a break. I had to find time to pursue my freshly discovered passions for helping others connect to their purpose and become the best version of themselves. In doing so, the joy I feel in playing a small part in assisting others in creating extraordinary lives, relationships, and businesses totally lights me up. When I could work only eight hours a week, many people thought I was crazy to start my company instead of seeking a job.

There were people around me who thought it was irresponsible of me to pursue my passion. They told me to accept my *new normal*. What I heard was they felt I should settle for an ordinary life. Thankfully, I ignored them, as I did everyone else who tried to discourage me. The negative talk annoyed me, and I knew it wasn't the right advice for me. Looking back now, my decision to move forward into the unknown and trust I could take one small step forward each day was absolutely right.

3) What Did You Love to Do When You Were Younger?

A simple way to learn what has the potential to light up your life is to rewind the clock. Before *they* got to us with their expectations and advice, most of us knew exactly what we wanted and thought of the future without constraint.

Were you obsessed with flying? Maybe you could schedule a discovery flight at the local airport. Loved pottery or painting? Sign up for an art class. Were you the one everyone asked to organize fun activities? Think about stepping into a leadership role.

4) What Makes Time Fly?

When I worked on Wall Street, I would come in early and watch the clock throughout the day, looking forward to when it was time to be done and leave the office. Yet when I had a family in front of me, looking to build stronger relationships and use their means to make a difference in the community, I would gladly spend hours with them and not notice the clock.

Not surprisingly, my true passion is leadership coaching. In this work, I love the luxury of spending the required time to equip and encourage people.

What would you love to spend more time doing that you don't get to do now? That's a passion, and you'd probably benefit from figuring out how to do more of it.

5) Finding Your Passions Is a Fun, Joyful Adventure

I often see people approach finding their passion with anxiety and internal pressure. It is critically important to discover and engage in things that light you up, but it's just as essential to change how you think about it. Adopt an un-serious, childlike attitude of play, wonder, and adventure. Remember, you do not need to dig for buried treasure; you are merely discovering what is already there.

Create a list of the following:

A. Notice what you enjoy doing. Your goal is not to *get it right*. You are brainstorming; there isn't a wrong answer. This is a journey of self-discovery. You will be learning and connecting to your best self as you go through this process. Research on happiness shows learning and trying new things increases the level of dopamine in the brain, which increases contentment.

B   Notice what makes you come alive.

C. Notice what feels effortless.

D. Notice what you would like to have more time for in your life.

Now, look at your list and choose one area of passion and ask yourself: *What is one small step I can make in my current life to move into that?*

Think of the chart of assets and passions, shown above. You want to move the passion line to the right just one tick. Do this, and you will see your life start to change.

Benefits of Finding Your Passion

Passion is so critical because if you view it as a process, it leads to your purpose. This is the assignment that, more than anything, connects to your ultimate contribution to why you are here on this Earth. You have already completed the first step of identifying your passions by connecting to your purpose. Passion will always give you the key to *why* something is meaningful to you. You don't have to be coached when it comes to passion because you already have it. Your passion drives what you're looking for as a job and the culture you want to be a part of. When you work in an area of your passion, you get paid for doing what you were meant to do, something that excites you when you get out of bed each morning.

If you can get paid to do what you're passionate about, you'll never work another day in your life because you're not really working. You're doing what you would pay someone else to *let you do* if you could. Passion connects you to the *why* of your strengths, talents, and gifts, which is essential.

Once I understood my goal was to move toward a 10 on the passion scale, it unlocked my ability to move toward a 10-out-of-10 life. Your gifts, talents, and skills are how you function. When you can answer the *how* and the *why* of life, you're halfway home.

Passion Versus Values

Now, watch this: The number-one challenge in getting an accurate articulation of passion, oddly enough, is confusing your values with your passions. You see, passion doesn't necessarily have a value system. Passion comes from the heart, and your values come from your head. In the next chapter, you will learn how to connect to your core values.

You have to understand both your passions and values to bring them into alignment, or you will have little direction. Values are incredibly important, so important because without knowing them, you may tend to get mixed up about your purpose. You might value being able to see people get set free from whatever limits them. You want to see people's lives changed. You want to give your life to helping others accomplish their very best.

All those are real values in a sense for many of us. The problem is vague language. Many people I've worked with encounter problems when they start to mingle their values with their passions. In doing so, they don't create a clear picture of what they want deeply.

So, remember this: Your passion has to do with what makes you come alive.

Your values have to do with the ethics and
integrity with which you pursue your passion.

This is your heart speaking. This is your head guiding you. Perhaps you have a desire for significance. You might be tempted to do something unethical to get noticed, but in doing so, you would be living outside of your integrity, and that will pull away from a 10-out-of-10 life. This is where the alignment of passions and values is so critical.

Intersection—Gifts, Talents, Skills, and Passion

What are you ultimately called to do? The *what* of life is depicted on the vertical axis of the assets and passions chart above. It takes time to get clear on what you do best. The *why* of your life is your passion—that which drives you to take action and jump out of bed every day, exuberant to do what you do.

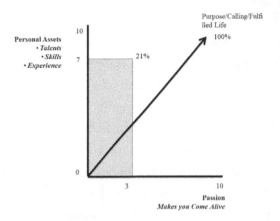

Next Steps

When you understand and have shifted your fixed mindset to a growth mindset, and you are clear on your identity, the third component of your True North is identifying and establishing your core values.

Identity Checklist

❑ Am I operating in my authentic identity or a constructed identity?

_____

_____

_____

❑ What are my gifts, skills, and talents?

_____

_____

❑ What are my passions?

_____

_____

Values

Your core life values affect every decision you make and, ultimately, the direction of your life. When you understand and work in your core values, you will develop an awareness of the life you have, the life you've already created. This will help you identify whether the values you have been supporting are pushing you toward where you want to go. If not, let's gain clarity on your renewed vision and goals in this chapter.

Have you ever been in a situation where you needed to make a significant work or life decision, but you just didn't know what to do?

The answer is finding and living out your core values. Let's first dig in and find your top core values. This will allow you to confidently and clearly make decisions and move forward.

A Story

It was 2004, and I was working 60–70 hours a week at a technology company, leading a business unit. We had just hit $100 million in sales and were continuing to grow. My team was always going the extra mile, supporting each other, and we loved working together. My wife was living her dream of being a stay-at-home mom of our sons, who were seven, five, and one. Yet there was a downside. I was on the road three days a week and always felt like I was not spending enough time with my family. Even when I was home, I was not present because of everything on my mind. Since we were a Fortune 100 public company, the stress of hitting our numbers, forecasting our business accurately, and working for a very demanding boss was taking its toll. I was sleeping five hours a night and had gained twenty pounds.

I didn't know what my core values were and frankly hadn't put any thought into what they might be. Each decision I made was informed by whom I thought I should be as a corporate leader, the expectations of my boss, and a focus on creating financial security for my family. I was performing at a high level, but every Sunday, I felt physically sick. The thought of getting through until Friday was almost overwhelming, so I focused on just getting through Monday.

My phone rang. An executive recruiter, who is a friend of mine, was on the line. He said, "John, I know things are going great at your company, but can I run something by you?"

My answer was, "Heck, yeah!"

I ended up taking that job offer in a completely different industry. At that moment, I was sure this was the answer to the stress and discontent I had been feeling. I didn't reach out to mentors. I didn't dig into my values. I looked at the new opportunity from the lens of what was best for me at that moment.

In hindsight, I wasn't moving toward something. I was moving away from something. I had lost sight of who I was and who I wanted to be. It was a situation I had created for myself because I wasn't honoring my core values or considering what my long-term goals and vision for my life were. Today, what I have found working with so many people in similar situations is that core values are the key to making important decisions. A mentor of mine, who is a master certified executive coach, told me that significant decisions and great coaching come from one place—working in your core values. Big decisions in your life need to be made intentionally by knowing who you are at the core and what you are trying to create.

What are core values?

Core values are a description of your character, how you behave, and who you are. They hold firm no matter what, even in times of stress and temptation.

So, why are core values so important?

Core values are a descriptor of who you are. They are your line in the sand that lets you know what you're willing to accept and not accept. Additionally, core values give you the guidance you need. They operate as an internal GPS for what you're going to do and not do. This is exciting because you can start quickly making crucial decisions when you know what your core values are.

We are going to follow the three-step process I use with each of my coaching clients so you, too, can find your own top core values.

Three-Step Process

Step One—Identify Your Values

Step number one is to take a look at a core value list. Sometimes they are also called personal beliefs. Just below this paragraph is a list of core values. Pick only the ones that really resonate with you. I want you to be careful. Please don't go overboard, circling everything that sounds great. Avoid the temptation to circle who you would *like* to be or who you or others think you *should* be. These are core values you live 24/7, the things that guide your decisions every day. Please use a pencil. You will soon see why!

Once you have circled the values that resonate with you, go back through the list again and choose your top three to five values. You may notice there are groups of values that feel like they should be together. You might find that philanthropy, community, and generosity are in the same category for you, and this could be described as the value of service to others, which would be one of your top core values.

If you find yourself getting stuck, here is a suggestion for you: Ask people that know you well, who have observed you during good times and bad, what they would say your values are. After a coaching session, a client of mine asked his wife and four children at a family dinner what they felt his values were and how important they thought each one was to him. He got some feedback that was incredibly encouraging and, at the same time, challenged his view of himself.

Accountability	Expertise	Practicality
Accuracy	Exploration	Preparedness
Adventurousness	Expressiveness	Professionalism
Altruism	Fairness	Prudence
Ambition	Faith	Quality-orientation
Assertiveness	Family-oriented	Reliability
Balance	Fidelity	Resourcefulness
Being the Best	Fitness	Restraint
Belonging	Fluency	Results-Oriented
Boldness	Freedom	Rigor
Calmness	Fun	Security
Carefulness	Generosity	Self-actualization
Challenge	Goodness	Self-control
Cheerfulness	Grace	Selflessness
Clear-mindedness	Happiness	Self-reliance
Commitment	Hard Work	Sensitivity
Community	Health	Serenity
Compassion	Excitement	Piety
Competitiveness	Helping Society	Positivity
Consistency	Holiness	Service
Contentment	Honesty	Shrewdness
Continuity	Honor	Simplicity
Contribution	Humility	Soundness
Control	Improvement	Speed
Cooperation	Independence	Spontaneity
Correctness	Ingenuity	Stability
Courtesy	Inner Harmony	Strategic
Creativity	Inquisitiveness	Strength
Curiosity	Insightfulness	Structure
Decisiveness	Intelligence	Success
Democracy	Intellectual Status	Support

Dependability	Intuition	Teamwork
Devoutness	Joy	Temperance
Diligence	Justice	Thankfulness
Discipline	Leadership	Thoroughness
Discretion	Legacy	Thoughtfulness
Diversity	Love	Timeliness
Dynamism	Loyalty	Tolerance
Economy	Making a Difference	Traditionalism
Effectiveness	Mastery	Trustworthiness
Efficiency	Merit	Truth-seeking
Elegance	Obedience	Understanding
Empathy	Openness	Uniqueness
Enjoyment	Order	Unity
Enthusiasm	Originality	Usefulness
Equality	Patriotism	Vision
Excellence	Perfection	Vitality

Step Two—Personalize your values

Now that you've picked three to five core values, I'd like for you to define them based on what they mean to you.

Remember, you're going to live by these core values 24/7. They are your line in the sand, and you will make yes or no decisions based on these values. For example, if you picked the core value "courage," what does courage mean to you? This is critical.

One of my core values is leadership. What leadership means to me is this: I always strive to positively influence others to create extraordinary organizations, teams, and relationships. I am always trying to think of ways to better lead—my family, my team, my Bible study, my clients— and I seek great leadership for myself through mentorship, meeting inspiring leaders, and asking them key questions and reading a lot of books.

For each core value you choose, you should have a list of reasons that light your fire to support your choice.

So, what are the core values you identified? List them below and write specifically what they mean to you.

Core Value #1 _____

Definition _____

_____

Core Value #2 _____

Definition _____

_____

Core Value #3 _____

Definition _____

_____

Core Value #4 _____

Definition _____

_____

Core Value #5 _____

Definition _____

_____

Step Three—Litmus Test

Now it's time to put your core values through the litmus test. This is an essential step. Let's see if the core values you picked are *truly* your core values. I take my clients through this test because they will often discover they have chosen core values that, when put through the litmus test, they realize there's no way they can actually support these values with their own real-life examples.

Identifying your core values is a process, and there is nothing wrong with going back and changing or clarifying what you have on your list.

Here are the litmus test questions I would like you to consider. For each core value that you chose, ask yourself the following questions. Think through these carefully.

Would you honestly sacrifice this value for money?

So let's say someone gave you one million dollars. Would you give up this core value to do what that person is asking of you for the money? This is not a judgment at all. It simply tells you what you thought was a core value for you is not.

Have you violated any core value in times of stress?

Think about this core value and how you have honored it, or did not, in the past. Have you ever walked away from this value when it was challenged or made compromises in this area?

Can you see yourself still passionately embracing this core value twenty-five years from now?

Core values are your essence, your inner being. This value isn't something that is going to change in two years, five years, or even ten years. This value is who you are, so you want to make sure you can still envision yourself holding this core value dear to your heart until your very last breath. Really.

Here is an entirely different perspective for the litmus test: *Could anything cause you to stop holding any of this value?*

What if, at some point, this value becomes a competitive disadvantage? Would you still honor this value if there is a personal cost?

Once you have gone through the litmus test for each of your top three to five core values, ask yourself this: Did I find a discrepancy in a core value and my own real-life examples?

No problem. Get out your pencil eraser and eliminate this from your list; it is not a core value. Go back to the list again and see what really strikes a chord with you, now that you have these questions in mind.

If all of your answers completely support your core value, you did it. I'm excited for you. You just found a core value, and you will be able to hold onto it through the ups and downs of life. It is truly who you are in your essence. I can't stress enough how critical core values are in making life decisions, business decisions, and personal decisions. Core values are a powerful tool to move you forward into what you want to accomplish in your life.

More importantly, you will stay true to who you are. You will not lose yourself in the twists and turns that make up life. Every day when you wake up, you will feel good about the decisions you have made and you will not wonder and question, *Should I have done that differently?*

When you discover your core values, you have power. In the words of Roy E. Disney, "It is not hard to make a decision once you know what your values are."

Keep Looking

Because values are such a vital part of the way you order your life and make the choices that take you down important paths, continue to work on this area. Work with a coach or share it with your mentor. Values will give you confidence to make the right decision with clarity. The next time you need to make a decision, refer back to your list and ask what value you are/are not supporting with each choice.

When you consistently honor your core values, here are some of the benefits you will reap:

- You will have additional fuel and fire to motivate action.
- You can make decisions with more clarity and find the best course of action.
- You will feel fulfilled and purposeful and have more joy.

Summary

Values are an underpinning of all your actions and your True North. Taking the time to identify and live out your values will ensure that you stay on track with your True North.

Use the Values exercise in this chapter to help you identify your core values.

❑ How will you continually measure your actions against your values?

_____

_____

❑ Going forward, what steps can you take to ensure your decisions honor your values?

_____

_____

Mindset

You try something, it doesn't work, and maybe people even criticize you. In a fixed mindset, you say, "I tried this, it's over." In a growth mindset, you look for what you've learned.
—Carol S. Dweck

Your mindset is like a filter on the lens of a camera. It determines how you view the world and all that is in it: those around you, your relationships, and your work. Once you know your identity and the values that underpin it, you can use that knowledge as a filter that helps you see exactly how your mindset is hindering you and helping you.

Your responses to events are shaped by your beliefs, attitudes, and assumptions. The feelings that are generated by those attitudes and assumptions inform how you react and process any given situation. This is all part of your mindset.

Mindset and attitude are the characteristics of the current mental and emotional positions from which you view yourself, other people, and events.

To understand your mindset, think about how you view and interpret situations and circumstances around you, as well as your own view of yourself.

Is your mindset:

- Negative, seeing only problems?
- Positive, seeing possibilities?
- Helpful, or limiting?

Why Mindset Is Important

Let's look at why being aware of the state of your mindset is so important and how your mindset can impact you.

Peter Drucker, the well-known business consultant and author, once quoted the Chinese proverb: *We don't know who discovered water, but we know it was not a fish.*

Our own thinking, our mindset, tends to be invisible to us, as water is to the fish. We don't know what we don't know. That's the basis for being unconsciously incompetent about something.

Mindset and attitude can often be the source of, or have significant impact on, your motivation. For example, if you are frequently fear-driven, it is hard to move toward your aspirations and goals. The key factor is whether you are aware of your own mindset and attitude.

Are you getting the results you want? If not, consider this: if you are hoping for a different result than you are currently getting, look no further than the mindset shaping how you view events, circumstances, and life in general.

In a Stanford University doctoral program, they studied 75 leaders of every kind and discovered that self-awareness is the key to success in accomplishing an organization's purpose and mission.[1] This self-awareness results in emotional intelligence within business relationships and decision-making.

A key to self-awareness is finding your blind spots. This type of self-examination may seem scary and not fun, but it is vital for shaping your mindset. Without awareness, you have no navigational reference. If you have no compass, your navigation system will not work.

Your mindset can shift you away from limiting beliefs toward the opposite side of that coin, which is liberating truth. The truth is you are uniquely equipped to carry out your mission on the planet.

Truth sets you free. To transition to liberating truth, take these steps:

1. Identify a limiting belief that might be holding you back.

   _____

   _____

2. Identify a truth in that belief that you can build upon.

   _____

   _____

3. Build on the liberating truth, taking small steps forward. One step informs you of the next step. When you make mistakes, you may get mad or discouraged, but it won't be the end of the world. What small steps might you take?

   _____

   _____

---

1   Toegel, Ginka and Jean-Louis Barsoux. "How to Become a Better Leader." *MIT Sloan Management Review.* 02 March 2012. sloanreview.mit.edu/article/how-to-become-a-better-leader/

Here's an example from my own life regarding changing my mindset by shifting from a limiting belief to a transformational truth. At one point in my life, I was harsh in the way that I communicated to my kids. I would get so frustrated with my son when I asked him to do something, like mow the lawn, and he would ignore me. I would get angry and shout, which just made things worse. My limiting belief was: *My children will obey me if they respect me as a father.*

I knew I had to make a change. I started to examine why I acted the way I did. I realized that I reacted in anger to conflict, and it had become a habit. After I figured out why both my son and I were acting a certain way, I had to *choose* to change.

The liberating truth is: *I earn my children's respect through how I act and show them love.* The next time my son ignored me when I asked him to mow the lawn, instead of getting mad, I asked him questions about how he was feeling in the moment and about our communication in general. I discovered facets of my son that I hadn't known. My shift in how I talked with my son totally opened up the lines of communication between us. Our relationship strengthened tremendously because of open communication and honesty. This paid off later in life when he made mistakes and was open to sharing with me, so we could work out his challenges together.

How to Make Mindset Work for You

One of the most important concepts I've learned is the difference between the fixed and growth mindset. This is a concept that was developed by Carol S. Dweck, who is a professor at Stanford University. She has written several books on mindset.[2]

---

2   Dweck, Carol S. *Mindset*. Robinson, 2017. Mindsetonline.com

People in a *fixed mindset* believe they either are or aren't good at something, based on their inherent nature, because it's just who they are. People with a *growth mindset* believe anyone can be good at anything because abilities are entirely due to their actions. This sounds simple,

but it's surprisingly deep. The fixed mindset is the most common and the most harmful, so it's worth understanding and considering how it's impacting you.

For example, in a fixed mindset, you believe: *I'm a natural-born leader,* or *I'm just no good at leading large teams of diverse personalities.* In a growth mindset, you believe anyone can be good at what they are called to. Skill comes from practice.

The fixed mindset believes trouble is devastating. If you believe: *I will never be great,* then when you have any trouble, your mind thinks: *See? I'll never be great at this. Give up now.*

The growth mindset believes trouble is nothing more than important feedback in the learning process. Can you see how this subtle difference in mindset can change everything?

Fixed Versus Growth Mindset Examples

Let's look at some examples of fixed versus growth mindsets. I've compared what you would do if you have a fixed mindset with what you would do in a growth mindset.

Gathering Intel

Write down your top five limiting beliefs. Be specific, especially as they relate to your dreams and aspirations. Place a checkmark next to the ones you are willing to give up, or at least reconsider.

1. _____
2. _____
3. _____

4. _____
5. _____

Make a list of three areas where you need clarity. Where do you need to get clear about what you want?

1. _____
2. _____
3. _____

Make a list of ten things you are grateful for right now. Be specific. Consider the various categories of your life.

1. _____
2. _____
3. _____
4. _____
5. _____
6. _____
7. _____
8. _____
9. _____
10. _____

Fixed vs. Growth Mindset[3]

Fixed Mindset	Growth Mindset
You want to hide your flaws so you're not judged or labeled a failure.	Your flaws are just a to-do list of things to improve.
You stick with what you know to keep up your confidence.	You keep up your confidence by always pushing into the unfamiliar to make sure you're always learning.

---

3 Dweck, *Mindset.*

You look inside yourself to find your true passion and purpose, as if this is inherently hidden.	You commit to mastering valuable skills regardless of mood, knowing passion and purpose come from doing great work, which comes from expertise and experience.
Failures define you.	Failures are temporary setbacks and learning experiences.
You believe if you're romantically compatible with someone, you should share all of each other's views, and everything should just come naturally.	You believe a lasting relationship comes from effort and working through inevitable differences.
It's all about the outcome. If you fail, you think all effort was wasted.	It's all about the process, so the outcome hardly matters.

How to Shape Your Mindset

Clearly, you want to cultivate a growth mindset. Changing your mindset is a process that requires intentional action. It starts with self-awareness. Choosing the growth mindset and acting on it will enable you to accomplish a lot more in life than choosing a limited mindset.

To change your mindset requires two things: first, recognize the need for change, and second, observe yourself to see if your way of thinking is bringing the results you want. I recommend to my clients that, every year, they read *Leadership and Self-Deception! (Getting Out of the Box)* by the Arbinger Institute. Some of my clients with significant mindset issues have had great breakthroughs after reading the book and discussing it in coaching sessions.

Self-Awareness

Self-awareness starts by exploring the ways you characteristically approach people and relationships. How do you define success in relation to people, events, and circumstances?

You likely view yourself as an actor, participant, or victim. *Actors* accept that, although they might not be able to control their circumstances, they can always control their responses to them. *Participants* believe that they are taking part in life in which circumstances control the outcomes. *Victims* feel like they are defined by what has happened to them in the past and don't take responsibility for their feelings, thoughts, or actions.

The category you fall into influences how you draw conclusions about events and experiences and why they unfold the way they do. Your category will impact how you think about your ability to influence. It will also affect how you evaluate the importance and value of people, situations, experiences, and results.

When you realize the need to change through self-awareness, then you can begin to watch and listen to how you interact with the world and all that is in it. Changing your mindset is a process. It takes focus and commitment to change your mindset because your brain is pretty set in its ways. If you have been in a fixed mindset for twenty years, it will take some time and commitment to change it.

Process to Change Your Mindset

1) Learn to Hear Your Mindset Voice

As you approach a challenge, that voice might say to you:

Are you sure you can do it? Maybe you don't have the talent.

What if you fail? You'll be a failure.

People will laugh at you for thinking you could do this.

If you don't try, you can protect yourself and keep your dignity.

As you hit a setback, the voice might say one of these three things:

I would have succeeded if I really had talent.

I knew I shouldn't have taken that risk. Now everyone will see me as less than capable.

It's not too late to back out, make excuses, and try to regain my dignity.

As you face criticism, you might hear yourself say:

It's not my fault. It was something or someone else's fault.

You might feel yourself getting angry at the person who is giving you feedback.

Who do they think they are? I'll put them in their place.

The other person might be giving you specific, constructive feedback, but you might be hearing them say:

I'm really disappointed in you. I thought you were capable, but now I see you're not.

Step Two: Recognize That You Have a Choice

How you interpret challenges, setbacks, and criticism is your choice. You can interpret them in a fixed mindset as signs that your fixed talents or abilities are lacking. Or you can interpret them in a growth mindset as signs that you need to ramp up your strategies and effort, stretch yourself, and expand your abilities. It's up to you.

As you face challenges, setbacks, and criticism, listen to the mindset voice and build on the one that moves you toward the life you want to live.

Step Three: Talk to the Fixed Mindset Voice With a Growth Mindset Voice

As you approach a challenge, you can answer the fixed mindset with the growth mindset. Here's an example of what that might sound like.

The Fixed Mindset (FM) says:

Are you sure you can do it? Maybe you don't have the talent.

The Growth Mindset (GM) answers:

I'm not sure I can do it now, but I think I can learn with time and effort.

FM: What if you fail? You'll be a failure.

GM: Most successful people experience failures along the way.

FM: If you don't try, you can protect yourself and keep your dignity.

GM: If I don't try, I automatically fail. Where's the dignity in that?

If you hit a setback, the conversation between the fixed and growth mindset might sound like this:

FM: This would have been a snap if you really had talent.

GM: That is so wrong. Basketball wasn't easy for Michael Jordan, and science wasn't easy for Thomas Edison. They had a passion and put in tons of effort.

As you face criticism, here's how it might sound:

FM: It's not my fault. It was something or someone else's fault.

GM: If I don't take responsibility, I can't fix it. Let me listen—however painful that might be—and learn whatever I can.

If you know certain statements pop up in your head, such as: *I can't do that,* or if you hear yourself saying something limiting out loud, be quick to change what you say or challenge that fixed mindset in your head. It takes constant and consistent effort to change the conversation in your head.

Some of the sayings you may have picked up in your life may be adding to the fixed or negative mindset without you realizing it. What you say may seem like it doesn't matter, but your subconscious mind takes anything you say as fact. Any time you say something like: *I'm slow on the tennis court,* or *My reading comprehension is slow,* you are telling your subconscious mind to carry that out. It's as if you take ownership of the thing you don't want.

I joke that, for years, I had an incurable disease, but I knew there was hope. The disease was foot-in-mouth disease. We can control a horse with a small bit and steer great ships with a small rudder. Your self-talk is rooted in your mindset and identity. Even the Bible has something to say about this, as we see in Proverbs.

Words kill, words give life; they're either poison or fruit—you choose.
—Proverbs 18:21 (MSG)

You have a formidable power within you. This power can launch careers and shape amazing relationships, or it can lead to abject failure and the destruction of relationships. Words have the power to harm or inspire hope. We must first become aware of our need to make a change. Change only occurs when the pain of staying the same exceeds the pain of change. Simple awareness helps bring a measure of restraint. We have to guard what we say, then choose to use words that give life.

Step Four: Act From the Growth Mindset

Over time, the voice you heed becomes your choice. Whether you take on the challenge wholeheartedly, learn from your setbacks and try again, or hear the criticism and act on it is now in your hands.

Practice recognizing both voices and practice acting on the growth mindset. See how you can make it work for you.

I had to make a conscious choice to develop a mindset that would guide me to the results I wanted to create, both in my life and in the lives of my clients.

Ask yourself this question: Does my current mindset support me in creating the future I want?

To determine where you are with your mindset, watch events in your life, how you think about them, how you feel about them, and what action you take. Think of a situation that you reacted to out of a fixed mindset and analyze what you were thinking and feeling that led to action. Then ask yourself what would be another way to react to this situation. Even if none of the facts of the situation change, your response to the situation can change. As you start to respond out of a growth mindset, your mindset will actually shift.

There is a children's book by an author named Molly Bang called *When Sophie Thinks She Can't* (Blue Sky Press, 2018). Sophie is a young girl who has trouble with math and puzzles, so she is very discouraged when her teacher announces that the class will be working on a math puzzle. Sophie just *knows* she will fail at this task. Then, her teacher shares something that will change Sophie's mindset—and life—forever. It is the word *yet*. Sophie and her classmates haven't solved the puzzle *yet*, but they will if they keep on trying . . . and they do!

What can you accomplish if you insert the word *yet* into your vocabulary whenever you are faced with a challenge? Act from your newly chosen mindset, and practice acting as if you lived from that mindset all the time. Create awareness of how your mindset is aligned with your True North.

Sometimes self-awareness is simply not enough. Notice people who have different mindsets from yours. Notice what those mindsets are and how they impact the person's actions and ultimate results in life. This is called the *observer self.*

When you access your observer self, you experience the moment differently. You can ask yourself what you learned from observing others. The observer self increases awareness and increases the choices for action.

Shifting your mindset has the greatest potential for your personal and professional development. Once you identify what you want to create, a major question becomes whether you have the mindset, the beliefs, energy, determination, and persistence that it takes to bring your vision into reality. Shifting your mindset to growth is one of the most powerful things you can do to get the results you are looking for.

Mindset Checklist

❑ Do I have a limited or a growth mindset?

_____

❑ What actions do I need to take, to move from a limited to a growth mindset?

_____

_____

_____

_____

❑ What have I observed in others and their mindsets that has impacted their behavior?

_____

_____

_____

_____

❑ What can I learn from my observations of others?

_____

_____

_____

_____

DESTINATION

Sow a thought and you reap an action; sow an act and you reap a habit; sow a habit and you reap a character; sow a character and you reap a destiny.

—Common saying

As a naval aviator, I was always fighting an enemy. Though one successful sortie might take us closer to the destination of defending our country, we never would reach a destination and stop. Pursuing the destination was ongoing.

What Is Destination?

When you intentionally look ahead to what you want,
it will shape your destination before it shapes you.

Your destination is the life you want to create, including both long-term and short-term goals. You must ask yourself, "Does my destination match up with what I am doing now?" My life was put on pause when I had my accident, but the blessing that came out of that trial is that I was forced to evaluate what was truly important to me.

Destination is the impact and contribution you make to the world. The pursuit of your Destination never stops. No matter where you are in life or what you have done, you always have the opportunity to move toward your ultimate Destination. You can choose to make a difference, no matter how old you are or where are you find yourself in life right now.

My wife Donna is a physical therapist who has specialized in geriatrics throughout her career. She has seen firsthand the dramatic difference in the recovery, vitality, and impact of the lives of her patients who have had clear destinations in mind versus those who have not.

Donna says:

> So many of my patients ask, "Are my best days behind me? What use am I to anyone anymore?" These patients are more difficult to motivate and have poorer recoveries and prognoses. Contrast them with my lovely and inspiring Great Aunt Muriel, who is 104 and brings joy and beauty into others' lives, still painting their beloved pets on feathers and canvas. She and my Uncle Charlie didn't stop living when their boys grew up and left home; instead they doubled down on living life to the fullest and making their Destination epic. They traveled the world and have influenced countless lives in their lifetime.

In *The Noticer,* by Andy Andrews, the main character speaks life and wisdom to a woman in her seventies who has given up on life and her own contributions and shares with her these six points:

1. God has a purpose for every single person.
2. You won't die until that purpose is fulfilled.
3. If you are still alive, then you haven't completed what you were put on earth to do.
4. If you haven't completed what you were put on earth to do, then your very purpose hasn't been fulfilled.
5. If your purpose hasn't been fulfilled, then the most important part of your life is still ahead.
6. You have yet to make your most important contribution.[4]

If the most important part of our lives is still ahead of us, shouldn't we get busy? No matter what has happened in our past, tomorrow can hold more joy, more success, more impact, and always, more hope!

Think about your Destination. What will you keep striving for your entire life? What destination is beyond where you are now?

Let's look at the components of your Destination. Destinations comprise your vision, missions, and flight planning.

Vision

Vision paints the picture of where you are going and why. You have to see where you are going to move toward your Destination.

Stephen Covey, author of *The 7 Habits of Highly Effective People*, said, "All things are created twice. There's a mental or first creation, and a physical or second creation to all things."[5]

This is why vision is so important, in terms of your destination. You have to see where you are going first, so you can determine what steps to take to move toward your Destination. The *why* of your Destination

---

4   Andrews, Andy. *The Noticer: Sometimes, all a person needs is a little perspective.* Thomas Nelson, 2009.
5   Covey, Stephen R. *The 7 Habits of Highly Effective People, Anniversary Editon.* Simon & Shuster, 2013.

is the motivator. That *why* is deeply moving because it causes you to do things you might not do if you did not have that deep sense of purpose.

Missions

Missions are those actions that tie into your vision. As Navy fighter pilots, we had an overarching destination to defend our country and our freedoms, but we had many missions within that. At one time it might have been to defend an airspace; another time, we would offer air support for boots-on-the-ground. All of the missions tied together to move toward the destination.

In your life, you have different seasons with different missions still focused on moving toward your vision and your destination. Your actions can shift in different seasons. For example, a person who feels their destination is to move the world closer to the cure for a disease might coordinate research in one season. In another season, they might have to shift to fundraising; in yet another season, they might be focused on raising awareness.

Flight Planning

Flight planning reveals what the road toward your destination looks like. I purposefully call it *flight planning* because it is ongoing, not stagnant. To prepare for a mission as pilots, we had to be clear on how we, as a team, would execute a mission. Intricate planning and articulate timing were always required to carry out a mission safely and effectively. Planning also helps when the unexpected happens because you can create a Plan B to mitigate your risk if everything doesn't go right.

This same planning is essential to move you through missions, toward your vision and big picture destination. How often you revisit planning will depend on the nature of what you are doing.

Know Your Destination

Even though you would not reach the destination and say, "I'm finished," knowing your destination keeps you headed in the right direction. You might decide to run an Iron Man triathlon even though you haven't been much of an athlete throughout your life. Even if you don't qualify for the Iron Man, you might end up in better shape than you ever imagined.

As a fighter pilot with the destination of defending the country and our troops, I was motivated to do things that rattled me to the core. Landing on the aircraft carrier as it pitched on the sea took lots of motivation provided not only by my will to survive, but also by the notion that I had a destination much bigger than that one sortie.

Knowing your destination guides you so you can choose missions that support your vision. If your vision is to be the expert on creating high-performance sports teams, your missions need to support that. For example, one mission might be to work as an intern under a great coach, while another mission could be to study the psychology of motivating teams.

Knowing the Destination helps you deal with ambiguity.

If you know what your vision is, you will know how to adjust your missions and flight planning when detours and hurdles arise.

Vision

Lose sight, lose fight.
—Fighter Pilot Motto

A pilot's visual acuity is key to their success. Seeing long range is important because of the lightning speed of the plane. I would travel from one place to another in a matter of seconds. The vision of what I was ultimately winning in a successful sortie compelled me to perform, even if my stomach and head were churning. Honestly, the vision of being a fighter pilot compelled me to leave working on the submarine to enroll in flight school. Others did not think I could be a pilot, and I had self-doubt, but ultimately, my Vision won.

What Is Vision?

Vision gives you the direction and momentum because it is beyond your current state. You have to see it to go toward it. Your *why* compels you toward that vision. Your *why* is the reason you are on the planet, the reason you do what you do. Your *why* is unique to you, based on who you are, what you have done, and how you are wired.

Your Vision and *why* may not change much in your life, but you can alter them over time. While the Destination you are striving for may not change, how you apply it in your life can change. Even though your Vision is basically stable, it may shift with the seasons.

At one point in my life, I had a Vision of a lifetime of serving and defending my country and its citizens. I always had a vision of being a leader. After my accident, the way I led changed.

Now, I have a Vision of helping people create an extraordinary life. I help them identify what they believe, who they are, and where they want to go, so they can fulfill their purpose in life.

Why Vision Is Important

Vision is the big picture of where you are going, and *Missions* are more tactical. Simply said, without clear vision you don't know what you are moving toward. If your vision is not clear, the missions within that vision cannot be clear. You could end up going in circles and not moving forward.

A pilot needs amazing vision. When you lose sight of the enemy, it's likely you will lose the dogfight. When the combat controller on the ground told me about a bogie within my range, I had to visually see the plane or call "no joy." If I can't see the bogie, I don't know where my target is. If I can't see the enemy, and he sees me, it's likely I will perish.

When I was flying at a low altitude, as low as 100 feet off the ground, the faster I went, the narrower my focus. At 450 miles an hour, trees, power lines, and canyons became treacherous obstacles.

Unfortunately, the faster our lives go, the easier it is to lose focus. We have to slow down to speed up. If you are going Mach 2 through life, you have to stop. You have to slow down and ask yourself: *What do I want my life to mean?*

Don't wait until you get thrown into a fence like I did. That accident stopped me in my tracks for two years. Fortunately, the incident led me to commit to what I really wanted to be. I realized the vision of my life was to be a *great* husband, dad, and the most trusted resource for my clients.

How to Get Clear Vision

So how do you obtain clear vision?

First, take it personally.

Second, do some self-examination. When you have done the work on identity that I described in an earlier section of this book, you'll see it plays into your vision. When you know who you are, it's easier to know what your vision is.

Take Vision Personally

Vision is direction for you, personally. It includes what you give, the meaning of your life, the best part of you. When you take vision personally, you can see everything about you and your life ties into your vision.

You can apply vision into time frames in your life that make sense to you. For example, you can ask yourself: *How am I taking my vision into the current (ninety-day to six-month) period of my life?*

A client was a partner with a major consulting firm. To get clear about his vision, he had to work to get in convergence with his vision. He was frustrated with his job and discontent was settling in. As he and I worked together, he came up with two options he felt would work for him. The first was to connect his vision to the work he was currently doing so he would be excited to go to work again on Monday. The second option was to pivot into a different company or industry. As we worked on his vision, it became clear to him he was at this consulting firm for a reason. His passion to help his clients solve real business problems while at the same time mentoring them to improve their personal lives was what he was made for. His *Aha* moment was he was doing what he was made for. Life got exciting again. Once he connected to his vision, he changed the nature of his volunteer work to be a mentor at his church and in inner-city youth programs. He was back to living life fully.

When you take personal responsibility for your life,
you know you have to take the step, even if it's scary.

You can transform your life by taking one small step forward. It takes courage to take that small step. Ultimately, that small step can take you toward your vision. Visualize what you would want people to celebrate about your life at your eighty-fifth birthday party. It's a way to project forward. What would you want people to say about you personally and professionally? I'd want to know I had an amazing marriage, and a deep relationship with my boys, and I had impacted clients' lives.

Self-Examination

Earlier you examined your talents, skills, experiences, and what you are passionate about. We are working to peel back the layers of Identity so you can meet the best version of yourself. The more you learn about yourself, the faster you will start to move forward. The following questions build on what you learned about yourself in Chapter Two and reflecting on these will help you slow down to figure it out. Set aside specific and devoted time to discover the answers to these questions:

- What am I naturally good at? For example, discipline with exercise, meeting new people, or entertaining people.

    _____

    _____

- What qualities do I have that stand out? For example, a ready smile, a caring attitude, or peaceful countenance.

    _____

    _____

- What do you enjoy doing? For example, speaking in front of a group, asking questions that cause people to think beyond the surface, or even tap-dancing!

    _____

    _____

- What are my talents? For example, athletic ability, naturally critical thinker, or master of finances.

    _____

    _____

- What am I passionate about? When you are passionate about something, just talking about it changes your demeanor. Something wells up inside of you when you talk about it to others. Sometimes you will go out of your way to talk about that subject or cause.

  _____

  _____

  _____

Make sure you write down your answers to these questions. Know that you probably can't do this in one sitting. It makes sense to record ideas about your answers to these questions as they come to you. In many cases it's helpful to have a coach or mentor help you with this part of the process. This person can ask poignant questions to dig down to things you might not have thought of.

Slowing Down

Some elements of your vision you will never accomplish. You don't just accomplish your vision once and stop. You are constantly moving toward it, and you may have to rejuvenate your vision from time to time.

At one time in my life, I was running my business practice with zero vision. I was running so fast that I didn't have time to figure out how to change. I had tunnel vision and a mindset of smoldering discontent. Working harder, faster, or more hours only served to increase my stress level. My discontentment slowly crept up on me over the years. I didn't know how to eject.

I discovered I could get to a different place only by slowing down.

I had to put on the brakes to re-examine my vision and how my life was playing into it. Only by intentional reflection could I figure out how to get to a different and better place with my mindset and life. In a sense, I had to slow down in order to speed up.

If you are in a place of smoldering discontent and not sure where to go next, stop, take a deep breath, and look at what you are doing and why. Does it move you closer to your vision? Even if it is valid work, or important volunteer work, if it doesn't move you closer to your vision, it may not be the right thing for you.

Next Steps

When your vision is clear, the missions that fit into that vision are clear. When your Vision is in clear view, you can easily determine whether any opportunity or activity that comes to you should be one of your Missions.

Missions is plural because they feed into the Vision. They represent the activities you engage in and the actions you take to move toward your Vision.

Vision Checklist

❑ How would I specifically describe my Vision?

_____

_____

_____

❑ Which gifts and talents feed into my Vision?

_____

_____

_____

❑ Am I in a place of smoldering discontent? If so, what will I do
to get out of it?

_____

_____

_____

Missions

When you discover your mission, you will feel its demand. It will
fill you with enthusiasm and a burning desire to get to work on it.
—W. Clement Stone

The movie *Top Gun* (Paramount Pictures, 1986) came out two years
before I entered my junior year of college. My new dream: to become an
F-14 fighter pilot. When I shared this with my friends and family, many
of them laughed and told me there was no way I could ever do that.

They said things like: Get real, Ramstead. Be realistic. You are setting
yourself up for disappointment.

I knew I would do whatever it took to accomplish this dream and
prove everybody wrong. After graduating from Rensselaer Polytechnic
Institute on a Navy ROTC scholarship with a degree in electrical
engineering, my vision began to unfold. I applied and received orders to
go to flight school. There were so many applicants due to the popularity
of the movie, we were told only one out of every 10,000 people who
applied would end up flying a fighter plane. My vision was crystal clear:
graduate number one, earn my Wings of Gold, and get orders to fly the
F-14 Tomcat.

When I showed up for my first day as a student naval aviator and I
looked at the syllabus, it was a bit overwhelming, to say the least. Flight
Training is divided into three phases. The first phase is primary flight
training in a turboprop, which has over a 50 percent washout rate. If

you successfully complete primary flight training, they add together all of your grades from ground school, deep-water survival training, and all of your flight grades to see if you qualify to apply for jet training. Only about 10 percent of the class qualifies.

The next step is training in intermediate jets, such as the T-2C Buckeye. If you can land on an aircraft carrier solo, you graduate to advanced jet training, flying the TA-4J Skyhawk. In advanced jet training, we study combat and tactics as well as land on the boat again. There are approximately 300 training sorties in all three of those phases.

My fiancée at the time (now my wife of twenty-nine years) and I sat down with a giant roll of white shelf paper. We wrote down every training sortie from all the three syllabi on that long piece of paper. It hung on the wall of my bedroom, and I stared at it every day. Before I would go to bed, I would look at that and ask myself: *Is there anything else I need to do today to succeed tomorrow?*

I had a definite purpose. I had a singular focus. Every training flight had become a mission to conquer. Naval flight training is one of the most challenging pursuits imaginable. Every member of our class was stretched to their limits, and what we were doing was so difficult, even though we were in competition with one another, our entire class worked together and freely shared everything we learned so we could all make it through successfully. I focused on each small step I had to take every day. I had a clear dream and goal in front of me, and this chart was my map for each mission. I knew what I had to do to execute it successfully.

Here is what happened: Through some incredible mentorship from skilled pilots in the classes ahead of me, a lot of hard work, and because I kept my vision in front of me every single day, I graduated number one, not just in flight training, but *in the country.* I was awarded the Chief of Naval Education and Training Student of the Year award, which covered all of the branches of aviation, submarines, and surface ships. I am proud to have that certificate hanging on my wall to remind me that to accomplish big things takes definite purpose, mentorship, and a laser-like focus on accomplishing a worthwhile goal and dream.

> *Instead of dictating what I was doing with my life, I was letting others dictate to me what I was to do each day.*

Fast-forward to my business life, twenty-plus years later. I had drifted into that land of smoldering discontent because I no longer had a worthwhile goal or dream to pursue, nor did I have a mission to accomplish. I want to share this with you because I know what it feels like to be in that place, to be running in circles, knowing time is flying by and the only thing different in your life is you are a year older. It is incredibly frustrating! If you don't have a clear vision, it is impossible to engage in any missions to support that vision.

What Are Missions?

In the military, mission is defined as, "An operation that has been assigned by a higher headquarters." Here's how that plays out: Say the White House defines the mission to liberate Kuwait. The U.S. Military's Joint Chiefs or the next level of authority down determine what missions individual units will have.

I was a pilot in Fighter Squadron Twenty-One, which was part of Airwing Five, and our mission was to provide combat support to clear the way for soldiers on the ground. The combat troops have the mission to capture a target, such as a village. Every sailor under command is expected to operate at their best to accomplish the mission. Understanding the mission and having buy-in greatly increases your chance of success.

Missions feed into your Vision. As you articulate your Vision, you can begin to see the Missions, which are activities or actions to support your Vision.

For example, if your Vision is to equip young people with life skills to help them take care of their families, your Missions could be any of the following:

- Teach life skills for earning money to millennials in prison
- Equip millennials in churches to lead their families in their faith
- Mentor millennials who have young families
- Create a program at a local college that teaches millennials how to develop job skills that pay a living wage

Missions can support other people and their Missions. For example, when we were providing air coverage for boots-on-the-ground, we were supporting what someone else was trying to accomplish. By the same token, we were supporting "up" because what we were doing was contributing to the Mission of the Joint Chiefs.

Missions are so important to you that you will do whatever it takes to accomplish them. Your commitment to a Mission is so strong, it's emotionally charged, which adds to your willingness take the actions that support the Vision.

Vision and Mission Intersect

Vision and Missions tie together like an ecosystem. My Vision is to equip and inspire leaders to accomplish what God has sparked in them. So, one of my Missions is to coach and mentor influential leaders. You might think you would find me carrying out that Mission by quoting scripture and talking about my relationship with Jesus, even to people who are not interested. Instead, I approach it much differently. The goal of every conversation, coaching session, and speech is designed to add value to that person. When 100 percent of my focus is on how to help others succeed, they end up taking small steps toward accomplishing their missions.

Connecting your Mission to who you are is a differentiator. Someone with the same Vision as you may have a totally different set of missions, based on their skills, talents, and experiences.

For me, coaching people one-on-one or in groups is one way I influence business and culture. My podcast, speaking engagements, and work with teams are other ways I carry out a Mission. Working on leadership training projects with the military is important to me because I served in the Navy and have a passion for our men and women in uniform. These Missions are based on who I am and what I represent to the world.

Missions can be small steps toward your Vision. The real key in determining Missions is making sure they are in alignment with your Vision and Destination.

Why Missions Are Important

If you don't make plans, someone else will make them for you.

If your Missions are not clear, you may go in circles and not move forward. Missions need to be carefully planned. If you are not following your own plan, you are just helping someone else complete their plan.

At one point, I joined a startup company, which turned out to be one of the most frustrating times I experienced in business. Instead of taking the time to connect the work there to my Vision and goals, I jumped right into the grind of chasing deals. This helped the founder succeed but did nothing to help me move forward from a paycheck-to-paycheck existence. Planning helps you when unexpected things happen—and they will. Like the time my wife and I had two little boys. The founder of the company I worked for couldn't pay a commission I had earned. We literally had to search through our couch cushions and penny jars to put a little bit of gas in the car and buy one can of formula.

Talk about stress! In the next chapter, we look more closely at planning and how you can determine what your missions should look like.

How to Determine Missions

Whether you are working on figuring out your Missions for the first time, or figuring them out after a change, the process is nearly the same.

First, you have to be really clear on your Vision.

Second, determine the short-term goal you must establish to take you toward that Vision.

Third, determine the small next steps you need to take within that short-term goal. Missions are those short-term goals that support your overall Vision.

Missions can change with seasons in our lives. After my accident, I had to figure out what to do next. I find my clients run into this situation too. I've worked with many clients to help them figure out how to make a shift into a new season. There are three options to pursue to figure out your Missions when this happens. These will work for you even if you are figuring out Missions for the first time, no matter how old you are.

Option One

Reconnect to what you are doing right now, but in a different context. Now that you have your gifts, your strengths, and passions identified, how do you incorporate them into your Missions? This will lead you to having deep joy with what you are doing now.

Option Two

What you are doing right now is not everything you need, but it is definitely part of it. What else can you do on the side? You could start a side-business. Maybe you join a board or volunteer at a nonprofit. The Halftime Institute calls this type of volunteering *Low-Cost Probes.*

Option Three

Make a complete pivot. This is what I did after my accident. I took a hard turn and went in a totally different direction. This was the best decision I ever made. So, my Missions changed because ultimately my Vision changed. I had to create those next steps that would take me closer to that Vision.

Mission Drift

Once you have set the Missions, it's possible to get into a rut and allow the Missions to drift from your Vision and your purpose on the planet. This is more prevalent than you might imagine.

Peter Greer has written several books; one of them is called *Mission Drift*. I interviewed him on the *Eternal Leadership* podcast. He talked about some intriguing data. Research shows, between our twenties and thirties, our satisfaction with life steadily declines and bottoms out in our forties. I mention this because sometimes you have to adjust your Missions based on the season you are in.

Your Vision to help young women and men support their families may not have changed, but perhaps you started a ministry as a Mission supporting that Vision. If you work in that ministry for many years and gradually realize you are not living fully alive and fully committed to that Mission, you may be in Mission Drift. If that happens, it's time to examine what you are doing and make sure it fits in with your Vision and Destination.

Perhaps you start in a job you love, and you feel it is taking you toward your Vision and Destination. You expect to stay there until retirement. Then, ten years later, you look up and realize you have drifted off into mediocrity and the Land of Discontent.

If you find yourself in that situation, possibly you have wandered from your True North. As leadership changes within an organization, you may find the company has moved away from a place that allows you to work according to your True North. This situation may cause you to drift away from your best self and drift away from your personal Missions. One day, you wake up, and you are in smoldering discontent, and you are not sure how you got there. The good news is there is a way out of smoldering discontent.

What's Next

Each time you have a Mission established, it's time for flight planning. We intentionally use the word *planning* since it is a continuous process, and it should have options for contingencies.

Mission Checklist

❏ First, write down a Vision you've previously worked on:

_____

❏ What Mission or a short-term goal could take you closer to your Vision?

_____

❏ What are some small next steps you need to take within that short-term goal?

_____

_____

_____

❏ What timeframe will you set to complete the first short-term goal?

_____

Flight Planning

> *Plans are nothing; planning is everything.*
> —**Dwight D. Eisenhower**

When we were planning a combat sortie, we had to consider a plan for our entire flight, which could consist of a minimum of two F-14s to an Alpha Strike that involved every aircraft on the flight deck. We were taking off and landing as a group. Each task within the mission took intricate coordination. We might have a mission where one pilot would bomb a particular building, another pilot would divert the enemy from the soldiers in the field, and still another would focus on crippling an enemy force. We had to plan which weapons to load on each aircraft. Then we had to think about what we would do if a plane broke down or ran low on fuel. And even with the best planning, we sometimes had a situation called *Blue Water Ops*. That meant we had to either land on the carrier or eject over water. This was because the plane did not have enough fuel for a land-based touchdown on friendly soil. It could be that to get to friendly soil, we would have to fly around an unsafe or forbidden airspace.

Blue Water Ops required split-second decisions in some cases. Once, in the middle of a severe storm, I had no option except to land on the USS *Independence* where the deck was pitching up and down forty feet—a very small target that was anything but stable. If I missed, my life and the lives of every sailor on that carrier were at risk. The image of the back of the boat coming up at me as I was approaching the flight deck is burned into my memory forever. I was terrified we were going to hit the back of the boat. The landing signal officer (LSO) on the platform near the landing area was on the radio with me saying, "Keep it coming; looking good," and I put my life in his hands.

Talk about giving someone complete trust! Thankfully, that trust was well placed.

Your Flight Planning

Though flight planning for your Missions may not be as complicated or include as many inherent dangers as a flight plan for a sortie, your plan needs to include the same elements. Your plans will include short-term, long-term, and intermediate plans. You need to consider all the tasks required to accomplish your Mission, how they relate to each other, what your contingencies could be, and how to deal with them.

Planning requires looking at all aspects of your Missions and how they tie into your Vision. So, based on a Vision of Equipping Millennials to Take Care of Their Families, you could choose the Mission of teaching men and women in prison to learn a skill that will support the family financially when they get out. Think of the planning that would go into that. You would need to consider these elements:

- Which prison(s) to focus on, and how to get access
- How to build curriculum or training materials for the training
- Key concepts and skills those men and women need to learn
- How to "make it stick" once they are released
- What psychological counseling might the men and women need to have the will and confidence to support their families
- How the program will be funded

Once you have considered all the aspects of a Mission, you need to look at waypoints and turnpoints for your plan.

Waypoints and Turnpoints

A common definition of *waypoint* is the set of coordinates representing the longitude and latitude of a given position. A waypoint is a physical location somewhere on our planet as determined by the satellites in the stratosphere designed for the purpose of communicating location data to a GPS receiver. A *turnpoint* is a place you need to turn to change direction to get to the next waypoint on your plan. So, even if you miss your initial turnpoints, there will still be alternate turnpoints to get you to your destination as you reroute.

These waypoints and turnpoints in your Mission Plan will help you navigate missing a deadline or other contingencies that might arise. This is like what happens when you depend on the GPS in your car to direct you where to drive. If you take a wrong turn, it will recalculate the driving plan and give you directions from your new location.

Planning for you will be different from someone else because you have different starting points, waypoints, and turnpoints, even if you have similar Vision or Missions you are trying to achieve.

Why Flight Planning Is Important

As you can see with waypoints and turnpoints, if you blow through your turnpoints, you have to change your navigation and course-correct to get back. Life is full of ambiguity, so using waypoints and turnpoints in planning allows you to deal with ambiguity. If something comes up, and it will, you have a map of sorts to re-route you back to your intended mission.

Flight Planning Process

Here are the steps to follow for your flight planning process:

1. Determine the outcome you want to achieve for a Mission. For example, "Create a new training program for Mindset Shift."

    _____

    _____

2. Ensure the Mission fits into your Vision. Ask yourself: *Will accomplishing this Mission move me closer to my Vision?*

   _____

3. Brainstorm a list of all the elements and action steps that need to go into planning and executing the Mission.

   _____

   _____

   _____

   _____

4. Organize the elements and actions in logical order and identify items that are dependent upon each other. For example, if you are writing a training program, you might need to create an eLearning, write a participant guide, design the overarching flow of the program, and record a video. From this list, designing the overarching flow of the program would need to come first, since creating the other elements are dependent on that. If the video is going to be a part of the eLearning, then the length and size of the video would need to come within the plan of the eLearning.

   _____

   _____

   _____

   _____

5. Create a project plan for completing the Mission, including dates tied to specific tasks. This should also include possible complications and their impact on the overall plan, and how you

would manage them. Here's where you can include waypoints and turnpoints.

_____

_____

_____

_____

6. Share the plan with someone who can find possible loopholes in the plan, then adjust it based on their feedback. This will also make this real and provide you with accountability.

7. Track how the plan progresses and identify learnings for the next Mission you plan.

What's Next

Flight planning is the final step in this Destination section. In the next section, you'll find help on looking at your Who You Are. Once you have figured out where you want to go, you need to consider where you are starting. Determining who you are will help you understand where you are starting. It's like where are you launching from.

If I were launching from the Indian Ocean, clearly my missions and flight planning would be different from if I were launching from NAS Oceana, Virginia, or NAS Miramar in San Diego, California. Once you know your Destination, the next step is to figure out where you are now.

Flight Planning Checklist

❑ Describe a Mission you have determined will take you closer to your Vision.

_____

_____

❑ Using the process in this chapter, create a flight plan for that Mission.

_____

_____

_____

❑ What contingencies, or things that could change or go wrong, do you need to consider?

_____

_____

PRESENT POSITION

If you are not in the process of becoming the person
you want to be, you are automatically engaged in
becoming the person you don't want to be.
—Dale Carnegie

During day operations on the aircraft carrier, we would stack up above the boat at 2,000 feet, waiting for the deck to "go green." This meant that the previous launch of jets had completed, and the ship was ready to recover the jets from a different launch. When an aircraft carrier is launching and recovering aircraft, it is on a predictable course. We were tasked with landing as quickly as possible. The goal was to land a plane every 45 seconds. As soon as the deck went green, we would jockey for position to be the first one to *come into the break*, or line up to land on the aircraft carrier. To land, we circled the carrier as the turns would slow us down, so we could line up to land on the deck. No one did this better than Lt. Commander Dave "Spanky" Spangler.

We normally came into the break at 320 knots, 600 feet altitude, directly lined up with the ship's wake to set up our "break" turn, which is a 180-degree turn we perform just past the bow of the ship to slow down and set up for our approach turn to the back of the ship. Spanky's signature maneuver was to approach the boat at 500 knots and 500 feet, and he would "break" just before the back of the ship. This maneuver is way beyond the capability of many elite fighter pilots. Essentially, he would come in at a 30-degree angle inside the wake, fly over the boat and slightly upward, rattling the bones of everyone on the carrier as he snapped the Tomcat into a knife-edge right over their heads. Nothing was more beautiful than the vision of that Tomcat, which looked like a supersonic dart with wings pinned back to a sleek 68 degrees.

One time, just as Spanky went into his break turn, it was clear something was wrong. His Tomcat rolled past 90 degrees and was almost inverted. The jet was rapidly losing altitude, and the nose was pointed toward the ocean at 400 knots. The radio erupted with "Freelancer 203 Eject, Eject, Eject!" Fighter aircraft are designed to be maneuverable, which is very different than a commercial airliner, which is designed to be stable. To help a pilot control the F-14, we had a Stability Augmentation System (SAS) controller. As Spanky went into the break, the SAS failed and commanded the spoiler on the left wing to deploy. Disaster was imminent. Spanky and his RIO had only a few seconds to pull the ejection handle. Any delay would have resulted in them being ejected into the water as the F-14 slowly rolled upside down, which meant certain death.

Spanky jumped on the intercom and told his RIO, "Standby. Don't eject; I got this." On the panels of the F-14 are hundreds of circuit breakers that control every system in the jet. Every other pilot in our squadron and I had memorized the seven critical circuit breaker locations that were part of emergency procedures. The rest we knew we could look up in our checklists if we needed to. An uncommanded spoiler deployment wasn't on the standard emergency procedure list. Unlike the rest of us, Spanky had put in the work to memorize every circuit breaker.

As his F-14 was rolling upside down a few hundred feet from the water at 400 knots, he calmly reached down to the panel near his left knee and, by feel alone, pulled the three SAS circuit breakers. He was then able to roll the airplane back right side up as the afterburners were starting to kick, about 60 feet above the water. The rate of descent was so great, impacting the water was inevitable. In an instant, the vertical speed broke and went to zero.

I immediately dedicated myself to mastering my craft.
I knew that I had come so far, and yet I had so far to go.

Spanky said it felt like the hand of God reached down and stopped the airplane in its tracks. The plane started to accelerate, and Spanky said it was like the hand let go. The nose rose above the horizon. They were able to climb up to safety, saving their lives. Later in the ready room, Spanky shared how he had saved the jet, his life, his RIO's life and the many lives of those on the flight deck at the time. I was in awe. I thought I was good, but I realized at that moment that I had become complacent. This was a starting point for figuring out how to get from where I was to where I wanted to go.

What Is Your Present Position?

Where are you really? This is a poignant question that can be hard to answer, especially with so much information that tells you where you should be. Think about how many influences you have or comparisons you can make to others in your same field. It's easy to get caught up with what everyone else is doing.

If you are not really clear on where you are *really*, how can you figure out how to get from here to there? Even if you think you are clear about your present position, self-examination and reflection are always good ideas. It often helps to reflect with someone else to help you get perspective. Here is where a coach or mentor can facilitate the truth about where you are.

Smoldering discontent, which I described earlier in the book, can keep you in a present state of status quo that doesn't move you toward your Vision. If you have the feeling something's not right, but you can't figure out what to change, it's time to dig deep into your present position. Ask yourself whether your current position is holding you back. Are you just going through the motions every day, doing what you have always done? Have you lost passion for what you are doing? These are all signs of smoldering discontent.

Typically, this creeps up on people. It's not like one day you are exhilarated all the time, and the next day, you are discontented. Life happens, and sometimes it can slowly move you off course in a direction you never intended to go.

Knowing Who You Are

If you are not clear about who you are, you will not know your starting point in moving toward your Destination. With so many people ready to give you input, and so many people to compare yourself to, you can lose track of your true identity.

In the cockpit, being clear about your direction can mean success or failure of the mission.

As a pilot, you have to trust your instruments because your mind
can play tricks on you.

I was on a training flight, flying the plane from the back seat
with my instructor in the front. I was flying above the clouds, and a
weather front was coming in at an angle, way off in the distance. I was
convinced I was flying to the right and descending, even though the
instruments told me I was flying *at wing level*, which means not turning
or descending. I started turning the plane to the left and noticed my
altitude was changing. I wanted to correct the plane according to my
instruments' indication, but my brain wouldn't let me move the stick
because everything in my body was telling me otherwise.

My instructor asked, "What are you doing?"

I knew immediately what was happening to me. I answered, "I have
vertigo. My brain won't let me move the stick."

My instructor took the stick and told me to put the instrument
hood on. When pilots are learning to fly on just our instruments, the
instrument hood blocks their view outside the airplane so they are forced
to fly the airplane with no outside reference at all. He then told me to
stare at the instruments and not touch the controls for the next few
minutes. When I took the stick back, he told me to keep the instrument
hood in place so I couldn't look out the window and get vertigo again.
At that point, I was able to fly according to the instruments rather than
the faulty logic of my brain.

Sometimes you may have to "cover your head" to
keep outside influences from convincing you that
you should try to be something you're not.

In your case, following what the instruments are telling you
could be input from a skilled coach, data from scientifically based

assessments, and deep soul-searching of your purpose on the planet. People who give you wrong or unsupportive input, or who want to tell you who you *should* be, often mean well, but you have to hold on to *your true identity.*

You might make false starts toward your Destination; that is a normal part of the process. They can slow you down unless you look at them from a different perspective. When you are clear about *who* you are and *where* you are now, every step you take becomes a learning experience that prepares you for the next step. For example, let's say you have discovered your Destination is to help people who have been wounded in relationships to rebuild their lives. You create your Vision, Missions, and Flight Plans to begin your work. If, after you have started, you realize you have not dealt with your own relationship wounds, you may have made a false start. Working on your own healing will help you to help others more effectively. This means you might have to delay your work and deal with where you really are.

In the next section of the book, we'll explore Self-Awareness, The Power of Association, and Habits. These are key components of understanding who you are so you are clear on where you are starting and where you need to go.

Self-Awareness

> *Strong people have a strong sense of self-worth and*
> *self-awareness; they don't need the approval of others.*
> —**Roy Bennett**, *The Light in the Heart*

My squadron of fighter pilots in the navy had a saying: *the arrogant die.* Though we were required to have courage and confidence in what we were doing, churning stomachs and heads were not uncommon. We couldn't second-guess what we were doing because of the sheer speed and the in-the-moment nature of it. A hesitation, a second-guess, could mean death.

And yet, we had to be humble about the massive F-14 we were managing. Being overconfident caused mistakes and cost lives. Any fighter pilot who was unaware of their arrogance while managing that plane could end up making foolish decisions. Those decisions sometimes cost their lives and the lives of others.

Your lack of self-awareness may not be physically life-threatening, but it can definitely be life-limiting. The true starting point for anything you do is awareness of who you are and where you are.

Are You Self-Aware?

Self-Awareness is about being honest with yourself. This is not always a fun exercise, but it doesn't have to be a drag. In fact, when you become acutely self-aware of who you are and how you come across to others, you'll find it can be very freeing. If you are operating with major blind spots, you may not realize how the blind spots are impacting your life.

Think about the areas in your life in which self-awareness is required. These include your relationships, work life, and spiritual life. These are key underpinnings of who you are and how you show up in the world.

Self-awareness is wrapped up in Emotional Intelligence. The book by that name, written by Daniel Goleman in 1995, has had a major impact on people around the globe. His definition of self-awareness is:

> *"…knowing one's internal states,*
> *preference, resources, and intuitions."*

This definition shows the importance of your inner world, your thoughts, and your emotions as they arise. Self-awareness includes what we notice about ourselves and how we notice and monitor our inner world.

Self-discovery leads to self-awareness, and this has to be approached with a mindset of curiosity and humility—not one of self-judgment. As we notice what's happening inside, we acknowledge and accept who we are at our best, as well as the humanity of others.

Furthermore, self-awareness goes beyond merely accumulating knowledge about ourselves. It is also about paying attention to our inner state with a beginner's mind and an open heart. Our mind is extremely skillful at storing information about how we react to a certain event to form a blueprint of our emotional life.

Such information often ends up conditioning our minds to react in a certain way as we encounter a similar event in the future. Self-awareness allows us to be conscious of this conditioning and preconceptions of the mind, which can form the foundation of freeing the mind from it. [6]

Your inner game determines your outer game!

Many intelligent people are not aware of how they come across to others. This can be devastating to our relationships, careers, and interactions with others.

Self-awareness sometimes comes in the form of feedback from others. This can feel like ripping the Band-Aid off a healing wound, but it's sometimes necessary to move forward. Feedback from others can be helpful. Even if you disagree with the feedback, it can help you to acknowledge it could be true for the person who shared it with you. All feedback is relevant because it is vital to the relationship you have with others. Ultimately, you will need to self-assess your behavior in the moment to know if you need to adjust.

---

6   Goleman, Daniel. *Emotional Intelligence.* Bantam Books, 1995.

Why Is Self-Awareness Important?

Recognizing blind spots will enable you to move forward. If you are stuck, it takes an honest assessment to break through. Often, it can take multiple assessments as you take small steps forward and learn, grow, and change with each step. You may think people receive and perceive you one way, but how they view you could be totally different from what you think.

Every time my clients go through a 360-feedback assessment—receiving candid feedback from their boss, peers, direct reports, and colleagues—they discover good habits they can build on as well as blind spots in their behavior that are holding them back. One of my clients felt he was decisive and gregarious, and his team enjoyed working with him most of the time. During the 360-feedback assessment review, he learned he had turned his decisiveness from a strength into a liability. His team didn't always feel the freedom to speak up or share ideas. If they did, he was quick to dismiss their input and could come across as condescending. This had greatly limited the potential of the team. With this new awareness, he worked hard on speaking last, asking questions, and making everyone on the team feel involved and important. He was still the final decision-maker, but he used this awareness to transform how he led, which resulted in increased effectiveness of everyone around him. The entire atmosphere of the office changed as people started to have fun. *Bonus!*

Getting real about how you come across to people is the key to creating solid relationships. If you are trying to share valuable information with someone, but they think you are arrogant, your message will not be well received. You are the only one who is accountable to yourself and your True North. Finding and curing blind spots is a process. It doesn't happen overnight, and it is much easier with your wingman giving you feedback. You will make mistakes, fall into old habits, and get angry with yourself. This is why it is so important to understand why you are working on this area of your life. Your wingman will be key in helping you move forward when you get frustrated.

How to Be Self-Aware

As mentioned before, key areas for self-awareness are your relationships, your work life, and your spiritual life. Becoming self-aware is housed in giving and receiving feedback. Who is involved in this process depends on which area you are working in. There are two types of feedback: feedback you agree with, even if it's hard to hear, and feedback you don't agree with. Feedback we don't agree with tends to conflict with how we view ourselves. In the past, I would tend to dismiss feedback I didn't agree with. My friend Ford Taylor taught me all feedback is relevant because it is relevant to the relationship and how others experience us.

Here's a question for you. On a scale of 1 to 10, how skilled are you at receiving feedback you don't agree with?

Let's look more closely at these three key areas.

Relationships

Relationships in which you need self-awareness include your loved ones, friends in your personal life, and people you work or volunteer with. Think of a situation involving a loved one. It might start with that person reacting to you in a way you don't understand. So rather than ignoring it, you can notice it and ask a question or make a comment in a nonjudgmental way to start the conversation. Your loved one may give you some feedback about something you did or how you are acting. At that point, you can choose to receive the feedback and make a change or not. You may have many reasons for not choosing change. The other person could be manipulative or in a bad place that day. The point is you have initiated a feedback loop, so you are aware of someone else's perspective. If you continue to get the same feedback from different people, it probably means it's time to change!

Relationships are clearly going to be different in your work life than in your personal life, but both require dealing with people. In a work environment, people may be adapting their natural behavior to fit a professional situation. This can create challenges in how you choose to receive feedback, as well as how you develop the relationships that allow you to give feedback. Feedback needs to be given from a spirit of lifting people up, making them better, not from a place of judgment and criticism. People may not feel as comfortable in a work situation giving and receiving feedback, so you have to set up the situation as a safe place to share.

For example, let's say you are working with a new boss. Your boss might have an initial meeting with you to set up expectations for your working relationship.

In that conversation, she might say to you, "I want to have open lines of communication with you. If you feel like there are things we need to discuss, my door is always open." She might also ask you, "What are your expectations for how we work together?"

In this case, she is setting up a safe environment to discuss things. That does not guarantee she will want your feedback, but it is a start. So, in this same scenario, perhaps a few weeks down the road, you want to let your new boss know some of the things she demands are hindering the workflow.

So, you could say to her something like, "I'm committed to keeping our work flowing smoothly so we can meet our deadlines and continue to serve our customers. When I am assigned a surprise report to complete immediately, it stops me from managing the workflow. It would help to have advance warning about getting those reports together."

Here again, you have opened a feedback loop so you can have open communication and a strong relationship with your boss. Starting the feedback loop might be uncomfortable for you since you report to her. Also, you may be fearful she won't accept the feedback or will come back with feedback for you that you don't want to hear. Even so, taking this calculated risk will typically make you a stronger leader in the long term.

You can apply this same feedback loop with people you volunteer with, yet that has still different twists to it. Volunteers are not paid, and you are both working out of the goodness of your heart. You may also be working with someone who does not treat the work like a professional would, so you might have some challenges in the situation. Again, establishing open and honest feedback up front is a great way to lead beyond influence as you continually strive to improve yourself and help those around you become better.

Work Life

In your work life, it's important to continuously look at what you are doing, how it impacts you, and how it feeds into your Vision. If you are stuck in a job or work you dislike, it's time to look at why that is. There's no sense in dragging yourself to work every day and being miserable.

> *That is not to say you won't have challenges, disappointments, or negative situations in your work that you need to manage through. When discontent becomes the norm and not the exception, it's time to examine what is going on.*

In this situation, often a professional business coach or mentor can help you reflect on whether you are in the right place or doing the right type of work. The seasons for what you are called to do can change through the years. Slowly, you may become disenchanted with what you are doing or the results you are getting. This can lead to that smoldering discontent that is sometimes difficult to identify.

Coaches and mentors are trained to hold an objective view of your situation. They can ask poignant questions to help you in the self-discovery process or observe how you are operating in your work and give you some honest and helpful input. Skillful coaches and mentors are trained to listen with the intention of reflecting back to you what they hear you saying. Then, they can guide you in your decisions or choices about your work. Often their skillful questions help you dig deep into a situation, so you can see it more clearly and determine what to do next or how to change.

Spiritual Life

The spiritual part of your life is often what drives your Vision. If left unchecked, you can drift from values, identity, and inspiration in your life. Having a spiritual grounding is like the man who built his house on solid rock as described in the Gospel according to Matthew.

> *Therefore, everyone who hears these words of mine and puts them into practice is like a wise man who built his house on the rock. The rain came down, the streams rose, and the winds blew and beat against that house; yet it did not fall, because it had its foundation on the rock.*
>
> —Matthew 7:24–25 (NKJ)[7]

When you have based your spiritual life on a solid foundation, it will not be easily swayed by the opinions of others, popular thoughts of the day, or your abandonment of your principles and beliefs. Look

---

7   *Nelson Study Bible: New King James Version,* Nashville, TN: Thomas Nelson, Inc., 1982.

at whether or not your spiritual life has swayed. What else in your life has that impacted? If you have veered off track, spend some time getting back to center.

Journaling during prayer time is a good way to give yourself feedback on your spiritual life and how it is impacting all you do. Here, you may have spiritual mentors who help you in a way that's focused on your spiritual values, beliefs, and activities. The mentors might include a pastor, Bible study leader, or spouse.

Slow Down to Speed Up

One thing I have had to advise clients of—that also applied to my life—was to slow down to get perspective. If you are running around so fast you can't see yourself, blind spots are hard to identify. You can waste a lot of time, damage relationships, and become pretty unproductive if you are not willing to take a breath and reflect on your life.

If you don't slow down, your life might be suddenly halted the way mine was when I met head-on with a fence. That halting can come in many forms. It might be the ending of a relationship or a family unit if you are not willing to truly see yourself. In some cases, you could lose your job or lose your health. Are you working yourself ragged and can't seem to get your work done? Can your physical body take all the stress of each day, or is this a blind spot for you?

You can spend a lot of time doing all the work to articulate your True North, Destination, Vision, and Missions, but *if you don't self-examine, all this work could be a moot point, and you will waste a lot of time*. You can use all these leadership ideas to help you to find your *why*, what you are supposed to do, and how you are supposed to do it. Then if it doesn't work, you'll get frustrated with all of it. Determining all these things may even have worked very well in the beginning, yet you still need to continue to examine yourself in relationship to the environment around you, and in relationship to who you truly are.

The fact is, *who you are is the most foundational thing.* If your mindset is not healthy, you can't expect results. You have to slow down to take the time and put in the work to be intentional about moving to the best version of yourself. Why is John Maxwell one of the greatest teachers of leadership? Probably because he has spent a lifetime developing himself as a person and as a leader.

Next Steps

Once you have looked closely at yourself, you are on your way to figuring out where you really are. Next, you'll need to look at those around you. They can have a great impact on who you are.

Self-Awareness Checklist

❑ What area of self-awareness do you need to work on most? Relationships, Work, or Spiritual?

_____

_____

❑ What are your potential blind spots?

_____

_____

❑ Who can help you identify your blind spots?

_____

_____

Power of Association

You are the average of the five people
you spend the most time with.
—Jim Rohn

I had just graduated from college on a Navy ROTC scholarship and received my commission as an ensign in the United States Navy. The orders to attend flight school to become a naval aviator were in front of me, as I mentioned before. Since the movie *Top Gun* was fresh on everyone's mind, there was an influx of applicants for flight school. Of every 10,000 people who applied, only one person would end up flying a fighter plane. I knew the majority of naval aviation was made up of helicopters and support aircraft, but my dream was to fly the F-14 Tomcat.

Before I left for flight training in Pensacola, Florida, my father gave me some of the best advice I have ever received. I have followed this advice my entire life.

My Dad said, "When you get down to Pensacola, I bet there's going to be a student who is already there who everybody is talking about, the 'Ace of the Base'; that person will be blowing away the program and on track to graduate number one. Find that person, buy him a beer, and ask him, 'What are you doing so differently from everybody else?'"

What my Dad was telling me to do was this: Seek mentorship and actively search out and surround myself with people who were where I wanted to be in life.

The "Ace of the Base" in Pensacola was John Foster. His grades were better than anyone in the naval training command had ever seen. He was tearing it up. John shared his philosophy with me: It is not the best *pilots* who graduate number one, it is the best *students*.

He realized in the very dynamic environment of flying an airplane, we are challenged continuously on emergency procedures and our knowledge of the aircraft systems. The training scenarios continually change mid-flight. We are required to process, think, and make decisions very quickly in the cockpit. John dedicated himself to preparing for any situation that could be thrown at him while he was flying the airplane. He wrote down everything he was required to know on three-by-five cards. He then taught himself to juggle, and while he was juggling, he would have his girlfriend or roommates quiz him on sections of his note cards. If he got one answer wrong, he would redo the stack. Answering these questions while juggling trained his mind to recall information during a task that required focus and physical activity.

John also told me the class I was in did not compete with the class ahead of me for the coveted slots to get into the jet pipeline. He advised me to get to know the other students in each class and, before every flight, to ask the students if they could share insight on a particular instructor, so I knew what to expect. There were a few instructors who were laid-back and friendly on the ground but screamed at students in the plane to see how they'd handle stress. Because I "got the gouge," or found out the inside information ahead of time, when the instructor's altered personality emerged mid-flight, I reacted with a smile instead of becoming completely stressed out.

Following this advice, I ended up making the cut to fly jets and couldn't have been more excited when I was given orders to Naval Air Station, Meridian, Mississippi, to start intermediate jet training. I observed something very interesting during this time. I freely shared with other people in my class what I was doing and how I got such good results. Yet, few people wanted to sacrifice the time and effort to study with John, me, and others who were approaching training differently and getting different results.

What I learned in naval fighter pilot training applies to your life in business and whatever you do. Surround yourself with people who are willing to pay the price to achieve big goals and have the discipline to put in the required work. Seek mentors who have done what you want to do and follow in their footsteps. You can see how the power of association pays huge dividends.

What Is the Power of Association?

Humans are conditioned to seek affiliation through families and tribes. These groups band together and establish rules to create a sense of safety and belonging, fight a common enemy, or accomplish something meaningful.

You may have heard the popular term *tribe*, which is a term for the group of people you associate with. Your tribe might include people who read your blog or listen to your podcast. They can include followers from social media. They are people you influence and who influence you.

Finding the right associations with people can be trial and error. You may have a group you spend time with on a regular basis whose lives or priorities change. Or, sometimes your priorities will change, or you will grow in your life when others are not growing and learning. Assessing your associations with people should be ongoing.

There may be some you encourage and give the tools to change, but they fail to take action. They can become a drag on your energy. So, the power of association doesn't just impact you in terms of who you learn from or who influences you. People you are trying to help, friends, colleagues, and anyone you spend time with on a regular basis impact you.

Why Is Association Important?

My association with John Foster was truly significant in my success in flight school. If I hadn't been focused on being the best student, honestly, I wouldn't have learned as much and would not have been prepared for my first combat mission.

The Jim Rohn quote at the beginning of this section also answers the question about why association is important.

*The people you hang out with influence you even
if you don't realize it. Who you spend your time
with is too important to be left to chance.*

Are the people you are hanging around negative speakers? You'll find when you are around them, you may start doing the same things! Maybe those people are feeling sorry for themselves a lot of the time. Even if you don't take on the same behavior, they can pull you down and drain your energy.

How to Create Powerful Associations

To start with, you need to ask yourself these questions:

- *Whom do I hang out with?*
- *What do they talk about?*
- *What is their attitude toward life, success, prosperity?*
- *What activities do they engage in?*
- *Do the people I spend time with hold themselves to high standards?*
- *Do they hold me to high standards?*

The answers to these questions will give you a clue as to why some of the elements in your life go as you planned, and others don't ever seem to manifest. This does not mean you have to ditch long-time friends, but you might choose to spend less time with them or find new connections of strength to put in your network.

*Surrounding yourself with positive people who have accomplished
more than you will add to your strength and success.*

Think of a glass of water that has some silt or dirt in it. The glass of water looks murky. If you continue to pour clean water in the glass so it overflows, eventually the water will become clear. The clean water will overpower the dirt. The same is true with relationships. Surrounding yourself with *clean water* relationships will overpower negative or harming relationships in your life.

Mentorship

Mentorship is a key component of the power of association. A mentor is one who can share with you from their expertise and life experience. The right mentor can pull you up in an organization by helping you manage the landscape and guiding you through career moves. Sometimes a mentor will have more impact on your personal life than your business life. As a mentee, you also have the responsibility to hear what your mentor shares and convert it to usable advice. The best mentors I know don't merely tell a mentee what to do. They ask great questions to help their mentees think beyond where they are now to where they could be.

I had the chance to interview mentoring expert Diane Paddison on my podcast. Diane has an MBA from Harvard Business School and worked in the C-Suites of two Fortune 500 companies and one Fortune 1000 company. She founded *4Word Women*, which is an organization devoted to mentoring businesswomen. *4Word* holds various events and meetings for businesswomen, but one of their most powerful programs is the mentoring program.

Diane's mentoring started in corporate America where, she says of women she knew in the workplace, "I wanted to help women see what they didn't believe." That's such a powerful statement on so many levels. Sometimes you don't see potential in yourself that a mentor does see. In other cases, you may know what you have to offer business and the world, but you might not have the confidence to believe it and demonstrate that belief. The right mentor can see qualities and possibilities in you that you don't believe or can't accept.

Mentors typically have a broad network that will help you expand yours. Diane says like-minded people at Harvard and in her corporate life created a strong and supportive network for her. When you search for a mentor, look for people like these, who will challenge you to live to your full potential and God-given talent, and at the same time support your core beliefs.

How do you find a mentor? In Diane's case, she knew the CEO of one of the first companies she worked for had her same value system. She called him on the phone and just asked him if he would mentor her. He accepted, and he helped groom her into the successful executive she became. She says you simply have to find the right mentor, know what you want to achieve, and then, have the courage to ask.

Mentees have the responsibility in this mentor-mentee relationship to take the mentor's advice and take the mentoring relationship seriously. This is why finding a mentor who is like-minded, has the same value system, and will support your core values is so important. Often a mentor has many responsibilities pulling on them, so mentees need to respect a mentor is investing in their lives in a way that can have a powerful impact on their success and life. The relationship goes far beyond what any of us can learn in school or training, and it's customized.

Your needs from a mentor-mentee relationship may change with a new season of your life. After I had my accident, I needed someone to help me find new direction. The accident, which was a life-altering experience, meant that I was starting over. I needed someone to guide me through that experience and to help me dig into what I was supposed to do next in my life. You are never too old and experienced, or too young and inexperienced, to have a mentor.

The mentor can also learn from the mentee. Often, these relationships grow into long-lasting friendships that continue to impact the lives of both the mentee and the mentor. If you've never had a mentor before, think about how you can find one.

- What in your life needs to change?

  _____

- Where might you need some help?

  _____

- Who would be a good fit to help you with that?

  _____

Have the courage to step out and ask that person to mentor you.

What's Next

Whom you associate with impacts you in a powerful way and shapes who you are. Habits also impact who you are. In the next section, we will explore habits and how they impact behavior.

Power of Association Checklist

❑ What impact do you expect with regard to changing your association with people and organizations?

  _____

  _____

❑ What association changes with people and organizations will create the greatest impact?

  _____

  _____

❑ Whom do you need to connect with and why?

_____

_____

❑ Make a list of five people who would be great wingmen or mentors

_____

_____

_____

_____

_____

Habits

> *If you are going to achieve excellence in big things,*
> *you develop the habit in little matters. Excellence*
> *is not an exception. It is a prevailing attitude.*
> **—Colin Powell**

The Lexico dictionary defines a habit as "a settled or regular tendency or practice, especially one that is hard to give up." The reason it is hard to give up has to do with the way your brain is wired. Your brain is focused on efficiency so it likes to repeat behavior loops. Your brain hardwires your habits. So when it finds a repeated behavior pattern, it works hard to keep the pattern.

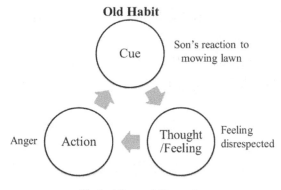

Desired Reward: Respect

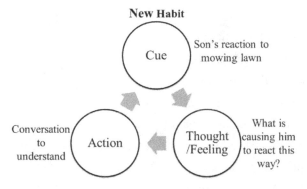

Desired Reward: Healthy Relationship with My Son

The Habit Loop

The Habit Loop starts with a cue or event, which leads to a thought or feeling, then to an action that has a good or bad outcome. The cue could be a teenager not budging from the chair when you ask him to mow the lawn. Your thought is: *He's not going to mow the lawn.* You feel disrespected and angry, so you shout at him. Obviously, that's a bad outcome. Imagine, as a parent, you have a habit that is hurting the relationship with your son. He might feel you are always angry, and the habit of getting into shouting matches makes your relationship worse. If you want a close and loving relationship with your son, you have to take responsibility to change this habit.

This was my habit before I made a conscious choice to change it. I had to change my reaction to the cue. I knew the cue would happen again. The next time I asked my son to mow the lawn, he said no.

Instead of choosing anger, I chose to remind myself of how much I loved my boy.

I sat down beside him and said calmly, "Son, when you said no, what did no mean?"

He was confused, put down his phone, and looked up at me. He explained he had practice soon and had to pick up a friend on the way. He hadn't really meant no; he meant *not now*. We ended up having a great conversation, and I explained what happens when he just answers no. We also explored his habit of saying no and how it was affecting his relationships with his teachers, coaches, and friends. I then asked him what was the best way to ask him to do chores that needed to get done in a timely manner. We agreed I would let him know about things that needed to be done and ask him when he would be able to do them. He agreed to this and followed through on it. This one change helped transform our relationship. My new way of communicating was very different from walking up to him and demanding he do the task immediately.

He and I had established a dialogue that led to a different result. I had been demanding respect instead of earning it.

To get a different outcome, you replace your negative habit with a neutral response of asking questions and giving someone nonverbal cues to start a conversation. When I made the choice to relax my posture and sit down calmly next to my son instead of allowing the anger to spread by staring at him with an intimidating expression, everything changed. The change in this habit loop requires a mindset shift. Instead of having the mindset that someone should respond a certain way, you can shift by asking what you can do differently.

For change to occur, the pain of change has to be less than the pain of staying the same. If I had decided not to change my mindset, my relationship with my son might have deteriorated even further, and I would probably have ended up having to hire someone to mow the lawn or do it myself. It might be hard for you to stop and think you need to change your behavior when you don't get the response you want from someone. If the outcome you want is a better relationship with someone, then the pain of changing is less than the pain of staying the same. You might have to swallow your pride and ask a colleague what works best for them.

Why Exploring Habits Is Important

More than 40 percent of your actions each day come from habits. What results might you achieve from examining your habits and deciding which ones need to change? Some of your habits could be beneficial.

Because your brain hardwires habits, once a habit is established, it's hard to replace it with a different behavior pattern. On the other hand, creating a new habit and getting it hardwired in your brain will mean there's one less concept or behavior you have to think about deliberately.

Your habits should work for you, not against you.

How to Break Habits and Establish New Ones

To learn about how to break habits and establish new ones, we'll look at how habits are formed, the nature of stimulus and reward, and how to unpack habits so you can substitute neutral or positive actions.

Habits come from stimulus and response. There's a trigger that begs a reward, either by avoiding pain or gaining pleasure. To change the habit, you need to unpack it by asking questions, such as: *Where does this action of shouting come from?* Shouting when you are frustrated and angry could be conditioning from the way you were raised.

Ask yourself: Why did I get angry?

Were you tired? Did you feel like the teenager disrespected you? It may not even have to do with the teenager not mowing the lawn. It could be due to a deteriorating relationship with your child. So, the *reward* in this scenario could be creating a great relationship and earning the respect from your son.

Here's another example. Let's say every day at three o'clock, you take a break from your work, go to the break room, and eat a cookie. After months of this, your waistline shows the results of eating all those cookies. Consider the reward for eating the cookie every day. You are either avoiding pain or seeking pleasure. You have to dig a little bit to figure out what caused your action and what pain you were avoiding or what pleasure you were seeking.

Why did you get up from your desk? Were you bored and needed a break from your work? Maybe your brain got stuck on something, so you needed a break to clear your head. It could be you like social interaction, so you went to the break room to connect with people— but you needed an excuse to be there, like eating a snack. The reward for you if you need social interaction is meeting with people and chatting in the break room. The cookie has simply become a part of the habit loop.

Let's say you have identified the reward for you is social interaction. You can replace the cookie habit with something neutral or more positive. Since the reward you need is interaction with people, you could visit with people at their desks or plan a coffee break at 3:00 p.m. just to catch up with someone. Now the cookie doesn't have to be part of the habit of getting the social interaction you need in the middle of the afternoon. Or at 3:00 p.m., you could take a walk around the office just to get moving. Before you know it, you could lose the weight you gained from eating those cookies.

So, you replace a bad reward of the cookie while talking to people in the break room with a good reward of walking around the office to stretch your legs and possibly visit with some people. The ultimate benefit to you if you lose weight could be a lot of things. You could sleep better, go hiking with your friends or family, or perform better at work because you stood up and got some blood flowing to your brain.

Any time you want to change a behavior pattern or habit, ask yourself: *What has caused this in my life?*

Once you have figured that out, you can determine what you need to change in your habit loop to break the negative pattern.

When you determine the reward you are truly seeking with your habit, then you can create a different outcome for yourself by choosing a different, nondestructive behavior.

Habits Versus Routines

Sometimes what we call a *habit* may be more of a *routine*. Why does that matter? A routine is easier to break. For example, let's say you used to go to the gym three times a week. Then you got busy with work or your travel schedule and stopped going.

You might say, "I just got out of the habit."

If it were truly a habit, you would be wired to do it no matter what. So to build a routine into a habit, you need to unpack it the same way you unpack a habit. What is the stimulus to go to the gym? The cue or event could be you feel out of breath walking upstairs. Perhaps you would like to go hiking on the weekends to get out in nature. The reward of going to the gym is you are able to do the stairs and not get out of breath, and you can easily hike around the trails on the weekend.

Extended benefits of that reward could include better health overall, which could help you sleep better and improve your brain function and overall happiness.

Next Steps

Taming your habits is one of the keys to making you the best self you can be. Any time you see yourself in a behavior pattern you don't like, stop and figure out how and why you got there. Then you can change your reaction to cues in your life. Take control of your habits rather than letting them control you.

Habits Checklist

❑   What habit do you want to change?

_____

❑   When you unpack the habit, what are the cue and reward?

_____

_____

❑   What positive cues and rewards can you replace the negative one with to cultivate a new healthy or positive habit?

_____

_____

❑   How is your mindset impacting the habit?

_____

_____

CONVERGENCE

Convergence is a phase of life where it all starts coming together.
—**Lance Wallnau**

C *onvergence* is about putting your True North, Destination, and Who You Are into an actionable flight plan unique to you. Like the catapult that jettisoned me into my first battle engagement, convergence will blast you forward, because you have done the work on your True North and Destination and folded in your gifts, talents, skills, and experiences. You have prepared for your first Mission like a naval aviator prepares for their first combat flight.

In one of the *Eternal Leadership* podcast episodes, I interviewed Lance Wallnau, a businessman and thought leader in leadership, and asked him about convergence.[8] He explained:

---

8   eternalleadership.com/media/podcast/eternal-leadership-podcast

God tells you to do something or gives you a vision, calling, or assignment. And, as you begin to make choices to move in the direction of the assignment, unusual and strange events take place that open a pathway to take the next step, and the next and the next.

I've found that when you reach a place of surrendering your life to the purpose for which you were created, you consecrate your life so you know and literally transact with God as you understand Him. You say to Him, I will do what you call me to do. If You show me the path, I will take it. At that point, you start to get visited in your imagination with ideas, problems that bother you, that are coming to you, that you'll find that you're ordained to solve.[9]

As Lance explained, this convergence pulls together everything under the umbrella of your purpose in life. You witness God at work when you are willing to do your part, take the steps to move toward your True North and Destination, and live as who you are created to be.

Why Convergence Is Important

Convergence enables you to apply what you have learned in this book and ensure its value to you. Convergence creates more than the sum of its parts in terms of sending you forward toward your True North and Destiny.

The combination of True North, Destiny, and Who You Are is much more than its sum. It creates an exponential result.

When you have convergence of all these things, you move into alignment with *why* you were put on the planet. Then ideas, network contacts, and resources will start to come to you. That is the magic of convergence.

---

9   Eternal Leadership Summit Podcast. EternalLeadership.com/12

For our purposes in this book, convergence consists of three key elements:

The first one is The Most Important Question (TMIQ), which is: What do you need to be working on to increase your influence and impact?

The second one is determining small steps you need to take to get moving in the right direction. This will keep you from getting overwhelmed.

The third is the OODA. This is a continuous improvement loop we used as aviators, which consists of Observe-Orient-Decide-Act! We will apply this OODA process to your life and work.

The Most Important Question

If you do not know how to ask the
right question, you discover nothing.
—**W. Edwards Deming**, Quality Thought Leader

Asking the right questions is key for most things you do in life. Learning to ask the right questions will make a monumental difference in what you discover in life, what you accomplish, and how well you stay on track toward your Destination.

The Most Important Question (TMIQ) is pretty simple. Right now, you may feel like there is so much to do to operate in your True North, to pursue your Destination, and to articulate Who You Are.

The starting place is the question: What is the one thing you need to be working on to increase your influence and impact?

You may have to ask several questions to get the answer. Think about:

- What one thing could you work on that would make everything else easier?

- Where will you influence and create the most impact?
- What is the one thing that will increase your influence, impact, joy, and relationships?

For example, if you are trying to build a following for your cause of providing clean water to those who don't have it, what can you do to create the most impact and influence? For you, it might be building an alliance with a group that is already connected with countries that need a clean water source.

Here are some questions you might ask yourself:

- *How does this tie into my True North?*
- *How does it impact my journey toward my Destination?*
- *How does it tie into who I am or my authentic self?*
- *What joy will it bring to me to make a difference for the people who need clean water?*
- *How will moving toward my Destination impact my relationships with family, friends, and colleagues?*

When you answer all these questions, you may discover allying with an organization that shares your passions has extended benefits. Working with another group will most likely make reaching your goals easier. Your influence will increase because you are not trying to do it alone. You are leveraging an organization that has already put some things in place. You will have a greater impact on the problem—again, because you are not trying to do it alone. And, you can expand on the connections of the group you created the alliance with.

Let's look at the personal benefits you receive by making this alliance. You may feel more joy because you see this will make it easier for you to fulfill your calling. Feeling more joy will likely spill over into your relationships, making them more enriching. The joy will give you more energy for your relationships too. Making this alliance will move you to live life more fully alive because you are using your gifts and following your passion.

When you have a win, you are making progress. To encourage yourself, track your stats on how your actions keep you moving forward.

Celebrate a win and remember something that seems like a failure can be a win if you learn from it.

In the above example, you may have to contact fifteen organizations before you find one you can create an alliance with. With each of those contacts, you might learn something about how to approach the organization, whom to talk to, and what to say. Even though a *no* may have felt like a rejection, it's a learning experience for you.

Self-Coaching Exercise
- What actions have you been taking that are moving you forward toward your goal?
- How can you ensure you will continue these actions?
- Can you improve upon them?
- What steps have you tried that have failed, or felt like failures?
- What have you learned from this?
- How can you turn this lesson into another positive action step to get you where you want to go?

Why Asking TMIQ Is Important
Asking TMIQ moves you closer to your Vision and what your actions would give you personally. You can move forward more quickly

by picking actions that create the most impact and influence. The influence could be over your processes and results or over other people you need to help you along the journey.

The lynchpin on an axle holds the tire in a place so it can operate and move forward. The TMIQ is a lynchpin for other things you do to get started toward your Destination. It converges all that goes into taking the right actions to move toward your Destination.

When you intentionally follow the path of most impact and influence, you have the psychological advantage of making progress, which motivates you even further. The small wins early on can drive you to achieve more. This naturally gives you more joy and satisfaction because you can see progress.

If you don't get a win in an area, you can reassess. Maybe you scrap what you are doing and try a different approach. This will keep you moving forward.

Process to Answer TMIQ

Here's a thought process to answer the TMIQ. Observe where you are trying to go versus where you are now.

1. *Where am I now in relationship to moving toward my Destination?*
2. *What is my Vision?*
3. *What are possible Missions under that Vision?*
4. *What is the first step I can take toward achieving the first Mission?*
5. *Next Steps*

Once you answer TMIQ, you can identify the first small steps to take. This will help you psychologically because when you have a small victory, a little win, it motivates you to the next action. It keeps you from getting overwhelmed in the process.

TMIQ Checklist

❑ What Mission fits into your Vision?

_____

_____

❑ How can you increase your impact and influence to move toward your Vision?

_____

_____

❑ How will taking the action above impact your feeling of satisfaction, joy, and relationship?

_____

_____

Small Steps Forward

That's one small step for man, one giant leap for mankind.
—**Neil Armstrong**, as he stepped on the moon's surface, July 1969

What do you do when you feel completely overwhelmed? As I was recovering from my accident, I spent more than two years total in intensive care and at a specialty hospital for the treatment of my severe traumatic brain injury. I also had twenty-three surgeries and procedures during this time, and my left eye was completely blind.

We had no income during that entire time and had drained all of our financial resources. My network had gone completely dormant, except for a few close friends who stayed in touch. I was in bed continually, recovering from yet another surgery. Also, I was in constant pain. Through all this, my vision became crystal clear. I saw my purpose would be to equip and inspire leaders to accomplish what is awakened in them.

This vision wholly resonated with my soul. It gave me the passion, the energy, and the desire to move forward. The only way to move forward was to break goals down into small steps. My first small step was to figure out how I was going to equip and inspire leaders. I hired a coach. The experience changed my life by bringing everything together into convergence. For the first time, I felt everything was in alignment, and my level of peace and joy rose dramatically. Convergence for me helped me see the purpose in every decision I made and led to living life fully. Because of that life-changing experience, I decided to become a coach, a catalyst in the lives of others. My next small step was to become a certified executive and leadership coach.

Another small step was to reach out to people I wanted to work with, interview them, and take fifteen or twenty minutes of their time to understand their urgent needs and their compelling desires. For me, this was a massive step in faith. Because of my injuries and complications, I could only work ten hours per week. I had no energy because of my traumatic brain injury and chronic pain. Every day was a choice to keep moving forward.

The next small step I took was to reach out every week to try to meet with two people and have a conversation about how I could serve them as their coach. I would get up in the morning and have an eight o'clock meeting. Then, I would have to nap in my car for an hour. I would have a second meeting. Afterward, I would have to go home and spend the rest of the day in bed. That was it—all the energy I had. In my condition, I don't think I would have been voted most likely to succeed as a new entrepreneur! My faith in God and passion for my Vision kept me taking each next small step.

I took this last small step every week, over, and over, and over. At the end of six months, I had eight coaching clients and was able to pay my family's bills and not go backward for the first time since the accident. Six months later, I had fourteen clients, and now we were able to not only cover our bills but to start paying off debt, give a little money to worthy causes, and invest in our growing company.

I have become a massive fan of determination and taking small steps. I have found when I start simple and small, things can grow beyond my wildest dreams. They can become epic. When I start too big, with an elaborate plan and something huge, I usually end up with something small, and I have to start over.

To get started toward your Destination, you need to take action. Planning out two or three small objectives, which are housed in your Missions, will move you down the path to action. Inertia can be a challenge when you have big dreams and accomplishments in front of you. Inertia works on an object to keep it in the same state.

Once an external force moves on the object, the object tends to move. This applies to all we do in life. Do you need to mow the lawn, but you've been sitting on the couch all day? Stand up and walk around, and it will be easier to pull that mower out of the garage and get after it! That's an example of conquering inertia.

Why the Small Steps Are Important

Small steps are achievable, which keeps you from getting overwhelmed and discouraged. Achieving these small steps will encourage you to complete the next step. Your brain likes wins. According to an article posted on *mbgmindfullness*:

When you achieve something, you get a hit of dopamine. Your brain wants to repeat the activity to get more dopamine. Dopamine is a neurotransmitter often referred to as the *chemical of reward*. When you score a goal, hit a target, or accomplish a task, you receive a pleasurable hit of dopamine in your brain that tells you you've done a good job.[10]

It's a way of using your brain in your favor. Small wins drive you toward achieving your Vision and moving toward your Destination.

Clarity Versus Trust

People often ask me: *How do I get clarity? What do I need to do next? How do I do it?* These are questions I've struggled with myself. As I was trying to put together all the programs we are doing now, a friend emailed me a story that blew my mind.

There is an often-quoted story about John Kavanagh who went to Calcutta seeking time with Mother Theresa. He went for three months and worked at the House of the Dying just to spend some time with her and talk with her. He wanted to find out how he could best spend the rest of his life. When he finally met Mother Teresa, he asked her to pray for him, for something he had traveled thousands of miles to request.

She asked, "What do you want me to pray for?

"Clarity, pray that I have clarity," he answered.

"No," she answered. "I will not do that."

Kavanagh asked why.

She said, "Clarity is the last thing you are clinging to and must let go of."

He explained she always seemed to have clarity, the very kind of clarity he was looking for.

Mother Teresa laughed and said, "I never had clarity. What I've always had is trust. So, I will pray that you trust God."

I learned three things from that story:

---

10   Roman, Kaia. "The Brain Chemicals That Make You Happy." *mbgmindfulness.* 06 January 2020. www.mindbodygreen.com/0-23924/the-brain-chemicals-that-make-you-happy-and-how-to-trigger-them.html

The first is when you are trying to figure out what's next in your life, seek mentors—people who will tell you what you need to hear and have the experience you need to reach your goals. Here's something you can do. Just reach out to people who are your heroes and ask them if they would be willing to answer some of your questions. Seek those mentors, and simply ask them for help.

The second idea I pulled from this story is to ask questions and be open to hearing replies that kind of blow your mind. Being open-minded to some feedback may be a different way of thinking.

The third teaching I pulled out of this was really powerful for me. From it, I actually learned how to trust God and move forward. Everything we've built—from the podcast, to coaching, to our company's worldwide reach—we've built without always knowing what the next step was.

I'm stepping into this new season of my life, not having perfect clarity, but my whole motto is: *How do I take that next small step forward, trusting God with what it is?*

In a podcast episode with Jeff Goins, he said something profound. He said, "People think you need clarity to move into action." His philosophy is action begets clarity. And I thought that was great. Put yourself into action. Figure out your next steps forward.

What Small Steps Should I Take?

You need to complete two to three objectives over a ninety-day period. This will form daily habits to move you forward. Now you have something to work on that needs to be done in community for accountability. You can tell others what you're working on and why.

Here's where a personal board of directors or your tribe work in your favor, by serving as accountability partners. You can share with them what you intend to do, then regularly report what you completed.

Ninety days are a short enough time frame to keep you active, moving toward those objectives. Any longer than ninety days allows you to put off activities with the risk of not forming daily habits. As described earlier in this book, once a habit is formed, the brain takes over. Your actions essentially go on autopilot. Your brain works with you as a partner to continue to take action.

Keep It Simple

One of my podcast guests, Kevin Knebl, an international speaker and highly successful salesperson in several industries, says the key to his success is simplicity. Kevin says:

> *When you complicate your life,*
> *you work against yourself.*

The small first steps you take can lead to your success when you are consistent with them.

One of the points he makes to salespeople is if you don't have enough results, it could be you are not talking to enough people. And his process is about having meaningful conversations with people rather than trying to sell them something. Here are the keys he described:

- First, you have to have the ability to identify people who can do business with you or refer business to you.
- Second, you have to be able to start a meaningful, heart-centered conversation with those people.
- Third, once you find people you can do business with or who can refer business to you, all you need is a simple method to keep you at the top of their minds. You want people to know, like, and trust you.

The other key to how he lives and why he is so successful is very simple. Every morning he wakes up looking for ways to show love to people. He doesn't do it to see what he can get from them, and they can tell he is genuine. If you are taking those steps listed above, do it with a heart full of love. In terms of leadership, people will follow you when you are showing love. That love is an attractive trait to people because it stands out in the world and makes them feel valued.

Next Steps

Taking small steps takes you toward your Vision so you can see progress. Assessing progress to make sure you are learning and continuing to move in the right direction is key for your success. That's what we will look at in the next chapter.

Small Steps Forward Checklist

❑ What are the first two to three small steps you can take to move forward over the next ninety days?

_____

_____

_____

❑ Who is in community with you to help you be accountable and stay on track?

_____

_____

_____

❑ How will you know you are successful at the end of ninety days?

_____

_____

OODA

> *Observe, orient, decide, act. It's fighter pilot terminology. If you have the faster OODA loop in a dogfight, you live. The other person dies. In Silicon Valley, the OODA loop of your decision-making is effectively what differentiates your ability to succeed.*
> —**Reid Hoffman**, Internet Entrepreneur and Venture Capitalist

I was taught the OODA loop in naval fighter pilot training thirty years ago. It is so effective that it is still being taught to fighter pilots today. The same explanation and process have remained basically unchanged.

Here is how it is described in Wikipedia:

> The OODA Loop is a process we go through hundreds, if not thousands, of times in a single day. It is a process that defines how we humans react to stimuli. Colonel John Boyd coined the term *OODA Loop* in the 1950s. Colonel Boyd, known as the "Fighter Pilot who changed the Art of War," was an F-86 pilot and commander of a fighter group during the latter part of the Korean War. He believed when at a disadvantage, a competent pilot could still overcome that disadvantage by "attacking the mind" of his opponent. His observations led him to a greater understanding of human reaction time and the coining of the term. Colonel Boyd trained his pilots based upon his observations of human reaction time, and as a result, his pilots had a 10 to 1 kill ratio over the superior Mig-15s. [11]

Human reaction time is defined as the time elapsing between the onset of a stimulus and the onset of a response to that stimulus. The

---

11   en.wikipedia.org/wiki/OODA_

OODA Loop, which stands for Observe, Orient, Decide, and Act, is Boyd's way of explaining how we go through the process of reacting to stimuli.

First, we Observe. Keep in mind that, although we process approximately 80 percent of the information we receive with our sense of sight, we can and do make observations with our other senses. For instance, you might smell something burning, but not know where the smell is coming from.

Once you locate the source of the smell, you are now in the Orient stage of the process. You focus your attention on what you have just observed.

The next step is to Decide what to do about what you have just observed and focused on.

Finally, you Act upon that decision.

The OODA Loop is what happens between the onset of a stimulus and the onset of a reaction to that stimulus.

One thing that has held me back from taking action in my life is fear. In the documentary movie, *Free Solo* (National Geographic Society, 2018), Alex Honnold said, "The big challenge in free soloing is controlling the mind. You're not controlling it—you step outside of it."

When people talk about suppressing your fear, I look at it in a different way. I look at it as expanding my comfort zone over and over again. Walk through the fear until it's not scary anymore.

OODA Loop Process

The OODA Loop applies to the Missions you create to support your Vision. It's like the continuous improvement process used by many businesses.

As pilots, we were always taking in lots of information. We had to observe our current situation and form theories about what was going on. Next, we had to Orient by setting improvement targets and determining

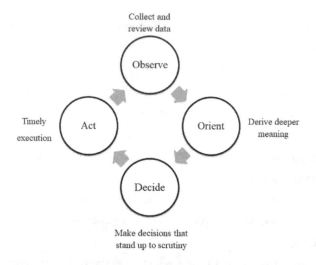

Collect and
review data

Observe

Timely
execution

Act

Orient

Derive deeper
meaning

Decide

Make decisions that
stand up to scrutiny

root causes of what we observed. Based on what we knew from Observe and Orient, we had to Decide by developing solutions. Finally, we had to Act based on the information and decisions. We then evaluated those actions and took them back to our observation input. As you can see in the model above, applying feedback based on actions is a key part of observation. The constant input helped us as fighter pilots to make the right decision during our Missions. The most poignant example of the OODA loop I can recall from my pilot days is landing the plane on the carrier at night.

Landing an F-14 on the pitching deck of an aircraft carrier is a terrifying experience. My anxiety about landing at night would start to build before I even took off. Imagine complete blackness. There is no horizon to see, just inky blackness. Then the catapult launches you into nothingness, and there is one dominant thought: I have to land back on the boat in an hour.

There was a study done during the Vietnam War that showed even the most experienced pilots had the highest level of stress landing on the boat at night. The study showed their stress was even higher than when they were taking fire from surface to air missiles and enemy artillery. The reason for this is they knew they have to land at 150 miles per hour on a moving target. To land safely, you have to put the fighter down in a landing area that is 45 feet long and 20 feet wide, so the tailhook would hook one of the four wires and bring you to a complete stop in fewer than 2 seconds. Your entire body is slammed forward into the harness worn on every flight.

At night with the deck pitching and rolling up to 30 feet, it takes every bit of focus and split-second decision-making you have. You have to observe your airspeed, throttle, glide slope, and your line-up relative to the centerline of the landing area. Next, you have to quickly orient relative to where you need to be to land safely. Then you have to decide what to do next and act quickly. If you are low, you need to add power. If you are above glide slope and your airspeed is slightly slow, that takes an entirely different correction. The approach is made without the benefit of visual cues because navigating at night is like flying through a black hole.

While landing on a carrier at night, I was making hundreds of corrections with my throttles, stick, and rudder. A series of bad decisions could result in catastrophic results. I was operating in fractions of a second. As soon as I took action, I'd start over. Observe what the act did; Orient to the new circumstances; Decide what to do next; then Act. To land safely, the OODA Loop played out many times per second as the back of the boat rushed toward me with my heart pounding in my chest.

You can use this same process in your business or personal life. Applying this process will definitely contribute to your long-term success. If you never assess the efficacy of your work, you won't know when to course-correct. That could lead to lots of wasted time and effort and lead to immense frustration.

Why OODA Is Important

> *The debrief is the most important part of any mission*
> *because that's where the learning happens. In the Navy, if*
> *we didn't debrief and learn, lives could be at stake.*

When you are using a process like this, giving yourself permission to fail is important because you might be frustrated, mad, or maybe even discouraged at times. Accepting possible failure helps you deal with the learning curve. If you learn to fail forward, or use what doesn't go right to improve the next time, you will always be learning and growing. And, the minute you are not learning and growing, you are going backward.

Sometimes in our culture, we put pressure on ourselves to always do it right. The trouble with that is if we don't make mistakes and learn from them, the learning isn't as powerful. The fact is, when you make a mistake and work through it to improve, your brain creates stronger neural pathways for what you learned.

I like to say you need to "get gooder" at whatever you do!

OODA for You

Here's a framework for you to use to apply OODA to achieving your Missions and moving toward your Destination.

Observe

Look at your current situation and the environment around you. What results do you see based on what you are doing? Consider environmental factors that might be impacting what you are doing. One warning, though: Don't dwell on things you cannot control, just factor that information into your decisions. For example, if you own a retail business, you can see many people shop online and expect free shipping. If you've noticed your in-store sales are dropping, you can use all this information to decide what changes to make.

Orient

Based on what you observe, how can you adjust targets? Do you need to change the way you do something, or change your marketing strategy? In the above example, perhaps you determine the root cause of dropping in-store sales is that fewer people visit a brick-and-mortar store for your product. Your new target could be online shoppers.

Decide

In this phase of the process, you decide what to do based on the observations you made and the resulting changing targets. In the above example, you decided your new target is online shoppers, so now you have to figure out how to reach them. Perhaps you use social media or build a tribe online who will support your business.

Act

Take action! It's key in this phase to make sure to track what is going on because that feedback will inform the Observe phase of the loop. As I mentioned earlier, the debrief is a key part of any mission, and that applies to whatever you are doing.

Next Steps

Asking TMIQ and planning those first small steps or objectives is key to get you going toward your first Mission. Once you are moving forward, and throughout all you do, you can debrief and track your actions to determine what adjustments you need to make. Now it's time to Break Your Personal Sound Barrier!

OODA Checklist

❑ With your first Mission objective, what did you observe?

_____

_____

❑ How did you orient?

_____

_____

❑ What did you decide?

_____

_____

❑ How did you act?

_____

_____

❑ What did you observe from the results of your actions that you fed back into the OODA loop?

_____

_____

BREAK YOUR OWN
SOUND BARRIER!

Great beginnings are not as important as the way one finishes.
—Dr. James C. Dobson

Y ou now have all the tools necessary to taxi to the catapult and launch off into a vibrant future. Hopefully, if you hadn't before, you now understand the power of having a wingman. In addition, I strongly encourage you not to wait until you feel you have perfected this process before you start mentoring your team members in this very same process on their own journeys.

Air Force test pilot Chuck Yeager broke the sound barrier in October 1947. He described the flight as a journey into the "Ugh-Known." Sometimes you might feel trying to break through to another level is an Ugh-known, since you are not totally sure what to expect, but you

131

still know you need to carry out the Mission. You know carrying out the Mission will move you toward your Vision and your Destination.

I experienced a lot of obstacles on my path toward my vision and destination; most of you have too. Press on. You can do this. My accident could have been a showstopper, but God used it to bring me to my life's purpose. Having to dig deep into my true identity, as I did after the accident, resulted in living my life more fully than I ever had. I am passionate about providing people with the tools they need to create an extraordinary life and get the results they want. I want to help people live their dreams, to find the disciplines they need to follow their God-given mission in life. I want people to know that even the life situations and events that don't look pretty or feel pleasant work together for good.

I'll never forget lying in my hospital bed, thinking: *I should be dead right now*. I started playing the whole movie of my funeral in my head. And you know, everybody says nice things about you at your funeral. That's what you're supposed to do, right? But then I asked myself: *What will people really say about me two or three years from now?* I had been so focused on the daily grind, ultimately resulting in the inheritance I would leave *to* my family. I realized I had missed a huge opportunity to focus on what I was leaving *in* my family and my circle of influence. This is what you call a *legacy*. Had I lived a life so the use of my life would outlive my life? I was given this incredible second chance, a second chance to rewrite my script. Here's what I realized: every day is a second chance for each of us. And guess what? If you missed it this morning, here's the good news: Tomorrow offers another second chance.

My left eye is blind, I'm in chronic pain, and it's been a long, slow journey back from this accident. Everything hurts and yet, *I couldn't be happier*. I'm at total peace. I've never felt more fully alive. Everything has been restored in my life—my marriage, my relationship with my kids, and my company.

As you turn the final page of this book, ask yourself one question: *What are you willing to do differently from everyone else to get the results that most have only dreamed of?*

Consider the questions I asked you throughout the book and go do some soul-searching. Take the time to answer the questions completely. Then, find that wingman to help you achieve all those things you formerly thought were impossible but can do with the help of a mentor. Next, pay it forward. Help your family, your friends, and your team to be wildly successful. Unleash their greatness and be great.

ABOUT THE AUTHOR

John Ramstead is an author, keynote speaker, trainer, former combat Navy fighter pilot, leadership coach, and international podcast host. John was named by *Inc. Magazine* as one of "The Top 12 Podcasts Leaders Need to Listen To." It is John's purpose and joy to launch individuals, companies, and government organizations into their full potential.

John grew up in Burnsville, Minnesota, and attended St. Thomas Military Academy. He loves technology, so he headed east to Troy, New York, to attend Rensselaer Polytechnic Institute, where he earned a degree in Electrical Engineering on a Navy ROTC Scholarship. While there, he met his best friend, Donna, who is now his wife of 30 years.

John's journey started when the U.S. Navy accepted him into flight school to become a Naval Aviator. The day he pinned on his Wings of Gold and received orders to fly the F- 14 was the culmination of a dream he held since childhood. He went on to fly combat missions in Iraq and was selected to attend TOPGUN.

After his Navy career, John became an entrepreneur. He was part of three tech startups, was on a Fortune 500 management team, board chair on two non-profits he founded, and has held many other leadership positions.

John was at the peak of his professional career when his dreams were shattered by a freak accident that, according to doctors, was not survivable. His recovery took over twenty-one months under hospital care and twenty-five surgeries. John had a personal encounter with God at the accident site who shared with him that he would be getting a second chance. With his life hanging in the balance, John emerged with a profound vision of how to live a life of significance. Since then, he has coached and mentored thousands of individuals and companies around the world. He currently lives in Denver, Colorado, with his wife and three incredible boys.

CPSIA information can be obtained
at www.ICGtesting.com
Printed in the USA
JSHW041628070421
13372JS00004B/163